(in)Visible

(in)Visible

From Obscure to Valuable

ARTHUR J. AMMANN

With
BARBARA McLENNAN

Barbara McLennan

RESOURCE *Publications* • Eugene, Oregon

(IN)VISIBLE
From Obscure to Valuable

Resource Publications
An imprint of Wipf and Stock Publishers
199 W. 8th Ave., Suite 3
Eugene, OR 97401

www.wipfandstock.com

ISBN 13: 978-1-62564-099-4

In my lifetime there has been an abundance of individuals who have blessed me and transformed my life's journey. They are individuals of value to me and in turn they have seen value in me. I am grateful to Marilyn, my wife, for her patience and love as a lifetime partner; my children, Kimberly and Scott, for what they have taught me; my grandchildren, Sophia, Caleb, Leland, and Avery, for helping me to listen to children; my friends for their understanding; my teachers for sharing their knowledge; and for the many individuals that I have encountered, many of whom are strangers, who have nevertheless taught me about seeing the value in another person whether educated or uneducated, rich or poor, famous or unknown. In all of them, when I looked deeply into their lives, I find the image of God. I also dedicate this book to Barbara McLennan, my co-author, who, through one of the very kinds of unexpected meetings described in this book, accepted the challenge of helping me revise and finalize the book, adding to it her own personal value and knowledge to increase its meaning.

My thoughts are often entwined with the mystery of the essential value of one person and our purpose in relation to a single individual. Is it possible for example, that our entire life—everything that we thought was important in our own spiritual journey, our varied ministries, our public service, our occupation, the relationships that we built, our education, and our professional development—might just have been a series of stepping stones in the pathway to meet just one individual of great value—an individual who will be transformed, or who will transform us, as a result of our mutual encounter?

Contents

Prologue

INVISIBLE

I am invisible—
a blur without form—
like a blue vapor mist
on a damp, foggy morn.
I am timid and frightened,
 sort of broken inside,
I am wounded and hurting,
so why wouldn't I hide?
I stay near the edges—
keep out of the light,
if people don't see me
they won't know my plight.
But oh, how I yearn
for a kind touch or a word,
some little sign
that perhaps I am heard.
My name is Refugee,
Orphan, or Stray—
the fifth of ten children,
or someone betrayed.
I'm divorced, I am homeless,
I have missing teeth;
my skin betrays me
of "foreign belief."
I'm a bell-hop, a bar maid,
any person who serves—
a snap judgment decides
if respect is deserved.

(in)Visible

Many eyes look right through me
not seeing my face,
though I have done nothing
to garner disgrace.
Come hear me, come see,
come learn who I am—
I long to be seen
as a valuable man,
or a woman with value,
 not just what I give—
what a difference it would make
in the way I could live.

—Barbara McLennan

Introduction

THE BEGINNINGS OF ARTHUR'S JOURNEY[1]

It had been forty-five years since I first began thinking about this subject. It started initially with a very short "book" of the Bible, one that the Apostle Paul wrote as a personal note, a "postcard" if you will. The idea that captured my heart and mind was a simple one, written almost between the lines of this brief letter. It stirred up a myriad of memories of relational experiences and principles that kept coming back to me over these past four and a half decades.

When I first discovered Paul's letter to Philemon I confess that I felt as if I were reading someone else's mail, a private message. (I even wondered if the letter, seemingly concerning just three individuals, had been incorrectly included with Paul's more extensive public letters and instructions to the newly formed Christian churches scattered throughout Southeast Asia.) I soon came to realize that it was included for people like me and it led me to realize that life really had to be about the value of a person. The more I thought about it the more I understood that there was something deeply spiritual and meaningful about relationships formed between two individuals, whether a close relationship of many years duration, or even a brief encounter with a stranger. I began writing down my thoughts as I saw applications of the principles emerging from Paul's letter. The connections multiplied and grew and almost unintentionally I began to realize it needed to be a book.

---

1. Throughout this book, the typeface used in this section indicates Arthur's words.

I realized that discovering another person's value also releases the power to transform me as well, in the way I live my own life. The lessons I learned from Paul's letter impact personal relationships in everyday life. In today's culture, when the value of the individual is under threat of extinction, it is time to think deeply about the great losses we face largely due to our own inattention. The principles formed from the story of Onesimus penetrate deeper and deeper into the unique world of our times, including technology, which descends over us like a dark cloud obscuring human relationships, imprisoning our very being behind impenetrable walls of isolation. Our everyday world is replete with ever expanding, impersonal technological communications. Our lives can be blown apart by just one electronic message devoid of explanations and emotion. Earbuds shut out conversation and signal isolation if not alienation. Increasingly, all forms of communication are brief and devoid of human sincerity. Advertisements intrude into our private space and overtake our senses. Others want us for what they can get, not for what they can give or discover within us. We are increasingly in need of learning to discover the value of a person through human interaction. Furthermore, we are surrounded by people who have bought into the myth that narcissism and technology will fulfill their deepest longings, but who inwardly yearn for meaningful relationships. These are the individuals we need to discover, to see, to hear, to touch and embrace, rather than retreating from them into the false security of an impersonal environment or the prison of invisible anonymity.

The challenge before us is bold and difficult. There is a price to pay for the desired intimacy we all need and crave. Personal change will be required, and change is tough, but the rewards are rich. Habits die slowly and the onslaughts of distractions are persistent. Internal fortitude is needed to stem the tide of devaluation of the individual, whether through technology or just selfishly ignoring them as if they were invisible. This change must happen one person at a time, a life upon a life. It all starts within each human heart and mind and the choice to lean in and listen to the life-beat of another human being. There can be no better time than now to embark on a journey of discovering the value of an individual. The personal rewards are great and there is also the potential of turning the tide against the many who would attempt to make invisible the value of the individual. My collection of stories and experiences remained on the shelf as if they too were invisible, waiting for the right time and place to be transformed into a book. The impact of a near-death experience turned the wish into urgency, convincing me that now is the time. A casual meeting of old friends at a Wheaton College class reunion and a vibrant conversation set the wheels in motion. A request for help in editing turned into a series of conversations and a writing partnership was formed that is now this book.

BARBARA ENTERS THE JOURNEY[2]

It was a simple request. "Would you be willing to read my manuscript, perhaps through the eyes of an editor?" But it started an unexpected and rich journey for me. From the very start, as I spoke with Dr. Arthur Ammann I sensed an importance and urgency about what he had to say and write. As his stories unfolded, the depth and breadth of his lifelong career as a pediatrician and immunologist, and later, his global focus on HIV/AIDS, emerged as highly significant and fascinating. It was also apparent that for Arthur a deeper concern was emerging within this global epidemic, the world's most drastic in modern times, affecting the lives of millions of people. Many of them were somehow in peril of losing their individual value as persons, to the point of becoming invisible as the world looked on. I soon learned through hearing his stories of personal experiences that his main theme is to always recognize and work to preserve the value of the individual person.

Arthur related his experiences of world travel and stories of people from diverse walks of life, including US presidents, leaders of the World Health Organization and United Nations, as well as powerless mothers and their children in some of the poorest and most remote regions of the world. As I listened, I became intrigued by the depth of his passion and the significant breadth of the unique accomplishments in his career of medical practice and research. Yet his humility and vulnerable transparency arrested me. His stories encompassed the personal as well as the professional, the societal and the philosophical, the secular and the spiritual, the ordinary and the unlikely. The whole of his observations and principles were clearly integrated and

2. The typeface used in this section indicates Barbara's words.

grounded in his lifelong journey of faith in God, which started for him as a high school student on the streets of Brooklyn. His faith foundations expanded and solidified through his Wheaton College years in the Midwest and finally culminated in California where he now lives. He has proven to be a "global citizen" as well as a humble servant of the underserved.

In spite of all his experiences and accomplishments, his attention is increasingly riveted on something different from the medical world he knows and in which he is so well known. Based on one of the shortest biblical books, hardly filling one full page, he has woven together observations and principles centered on the writings of another "older man"—the great Apostle Paul. Upon reflection, Arthur came to an unexpected conclusion: the main thrust of this brief personal letter is embodied in the ability to discover the value of a single person. As Arthur told his own stories, covering his decades of human interaction, he had me leaning in to listen, as one does when they realize an "ending" might be looming on the horizon. I soon learned that he had experienced a near-death event, precipitated by a cardiac arrest, but was brought back to this world causing him to reflect on the most significant values in life. Arthur found himself haunted by his call to complete this unfinished book, to tell his stories of how Paul's letter to Philemon informed him of the greatest potential significance in the journey through life. It is clearly the people whom we encounter that are important—not because of power, wealth, position, or prestige, but because of their own intrinsic value. It is precisely in this process of discovering the value of another that we ourselves are enriched and transformed in a unique way.

When Arthur asked me to help him put his story into writing I was caught off guard. "How could I possibly be of help to you?" I protested, "I have just entered this equation and you have been thinking about it for many years." He persisted with the invitation to enter a conversation with him, asking me to hear and probe and question the whole idea of "discovering a person of value." I soon realized this was an adventure I couldn't refuse—I felt compelled to accept the offer. I could see that these stories and insights were close to the surface of this man's mind and soul, waiting to be verbalized and transformed into a long-awaited book. Thus our team of two was formed.

A NOTE TO OUR READERS

We began our fascinating conversation into which you, our readers, are now invited to participate—a journey with multiple topics and directions, about people and relationships centering on the concept of "invisible persons" becoming visible and valuable. We welcome you to your own deliberation in the "Think on These Things" section of each chapter and to consider the questions through the lens of your own life and times. For all of us, the challenge emerges to discover the "invisible" person as valuable and participate in the process of transformation.

The Letter of Paul the Apostle to Philemon

Paul, a prisoner of Christ Jesus, and Timothy our brother, to Philemon our dear friend and fellow worker, to Apphia our sister, to Archippus our fellow soldier and to the church that meets in your home: Grace to you and peace from God our Father and the Lord Jesus Christ.

I always thank my God as I remember you in my prayers, because I heard about your faith in the Lord Jesus and your love for all the saints. I pray that you may be active in sharing your faith, so that you will have a full understanding of every good thing we have in Christ. Your love has given me great joy and encouragement, because you, brother, have refreshed the hearts of the saints.

Therefore, although in Christ I could be bold and order you to do what you ought to do, yet I appeal to you on the basis of love. I then, as Paul—an old man and now also a prisoner of Christ Jesus— I appeal to you for my son Onesimus, who became my son while I was in chains. Formerly he was useless to you, but now he has become useful both to you and to me.

I am sending him—who is my very heart—back to you. I would have liked to keep him with me so that he could take your place in helping me while I am in chains for the gospel. But I did not want to do anything without your consent, so that any favor you do will be spontaneous and not forced. Perhaps the reason he was separated from you for a little while was that you might have him back for good—no longer as a slave, but better than a slave, as a dear brother.

He is very dear to me but even dearer to you, both as a man and as a brother in the Lord.

So if you consider me a partner, welcome him as you would welcome me. If he has done you any wrong or owes you anything, charge it to me. I, Paul, am writing this with my own hand. I will pay it back—not to mention that you owe me your very self. I do wish, brother, that I may have some benefit from you in the Lord; refresh my heart in Christ. Confident of your obedience, I write to you, knowing that you will do even more than I ask.

And one thing more: Prepare a guest room for me, because I hope to be restored to you in answer to your prayers.

Epaphras, my fellow prisoner in Christ Jesus, sends you greetings. And so do Mark, Aristarchus, Demas and Luke, my fellow workers. The grace of the Lord Jesus Christ be with your spirit.

1

Value within Friendships

Therefore, although in Christ I could be bold and order you to do what you ought to do, yet I appeal to you on the basis of love. I then, as Paul— an old man and now also a prisoner of Christ Jesus—I appeal to you for my son Onesimus, who became my son while I was in chains. Formerly he was useless to you but now he has become useful both to you and to me. I am sending him—who is my very heart—back to you. I would have liked to keep him with me so that he could take your place in helping me while I am in chains for the Gospel. (Phlm 8–13)

Barbara[1]: We begin our conversation about the letter to Philemon with the verses quoted above. The sweep of this quote from Paul's letter sparks thoughtful commentary as well as touching stories from Arthur's' life on the subject of friends and friendships.

There are many relationships of great potential value, and we both have found some friendships enduring for a lifetime, but no less meaningful are those of even a brief duration—enduring because they are persons of value. Some friendships actually begin with seeing

---

1. Throughout this book the typeface used here indicates Barbara's words.

value within a person. We may define friends differently, but no matter what age, gender, position, culture or relationship to one another, it would be difficult to find anyone who has not in their lifetime identified at least several individuals as their "friends" and perhaps a few as "close friends" of great value.

LEVELS AND LAYERS OF FRIENDSHIP

Arthur[2]: The depth of friendships may vary, and we live in a time when a friendship may be considered merely a relationship that is one step above a stranger. We see in our highly technical culture that they may amount to nothing more than an accumulation of virtual "friends" on Facebook. This plays into the deeply entrenched myth that technology can meet the fundamental personal and spiritual needs that friendship provides. Going a step further, although our culture readily defines love as a transient physical attraction, the reality is that there is a difference between individuals whom we love and the ones whom we love deeply. So too with friends: there are friends with whom we form casual relationships and there are friends with whom we share deep emotional and spiritual values.

C. S. Lewis, a beloved British author, in his book *The Four Loves* identifies friendship as one of the four loves (affection, erotic love, love of God, and friendship) and states, "But very few modern people think Friendship a love of comparable value or even a love at all." He points out, "To the Ancients, Friendship seemed the happiest and most fully human of all loves: the crown of the school of virtue."[3] But in his time he felt, perhaps as we do today, that the world ignores friendship as something of little value. C. S. Lewis believed that few see the deep value of friendship because few experience it.

It is important to think about what true friendship means and to understand what was meant by the statement in the biblical book of Proverbs, "One who has unreliable friends soon comes to ruin, but there is a friend who sticks closer than a brother" (18:24). Few people understand how this level of friendship can lead to deeper and more meaningful relationships.

2. The typeface used here indicates Arthur's words throughout the book.
3. C. S. Lewis, *The Four Loves* (New York: Harcourt, Brace, 1960), 87.

A PUZZLING DIFFERENCE

We note that current studies in the field of psychology show differences between men's friendships with men and women's friendships with women. We both find this to be true in our own circles of relationships and a worthwhile subject to discuss.

The depth of a friendship may vary in relation to how we define or understand what having or being a friend really means. I have been envious of women and their friends. It is not that men don't have friends or that women always have friends; it is that men seem to have fewer friends and they rarely engage in the depth of sharing and understanding that women and their friends enjoy. It is an interesting question to ask a man to define friendship and compare his response to that of a woman.

Some of my observations on how men define friends are derived from such unlikely events as memorial services. I have listened to a number of eulogies from carefully selected men about their friendship with a deceased male friend only to learn nothing about the person other than the sports they enjoyed and a list of their professional accomplishments. It seemed strange that these could be the primary memories after years of friendship and hours spent together. The comments seemed devoid of feeling, emotion, and understanding. What of the inner person, his beliefs, his changing emotions through the years, his struggles to be a good father or a good husband? What of the value of the person to the man giving the eulogy?

This makes me wonder if another reason might be a man's unwillingness to be vulnerable and show his deep personal emotions in public. This commentary on male relationships brings to Arthur's mind observations about the greater depth of women's friendships and their ability to communicate.

I began to think more about the depth of friendships when I would hear a phone message in progress for my wife, Marilyn, or observe the ongoing flutter of activity among her woman friends. The particular thing that struck me was when I overheard statements like, "Marilyn, I have been thinking of you," or "Marilyn, I have been praying for you." What seemed to be expressed in those simple communications was concern at a much more intimate level than what I have experienced. I observed the friendships between my wife and her friends and concluded that women seem to reach deeper into who the person is, rather than what the person does, reaching an entirely different conclusion about the value of friendship than men do.

We compare notes about how few real friends we have in our lives, who care deeply enough to go beyond chatter, business language, and conversations that do not challenge emotional or spiritual dimensions—who instead reach deeply into the meaning of life, lay open emotions that pull us in new directions in our thinking, and instill value in a relationship. When these friends are found, they remain intimately locked in our thoughts as selfless beings who give love because they see value in us but demand nothing in return. They are rare treasures.

Because we are important to true friends, they do not attempt to control our decisions—they see in us value that is not seen by others. True friendship helps us to overcome our frailties and build our strengths. You know they are true friends because they are always there, prepared to understand and encourage and seek out the value within, often putting aside their own needs. In fact this brings to mind the most significant friendship of my youth, one whose probing question changed the course of my life.

A FRIEND NAMED FRED

My first true friend was Fred Bornholt, a friendship incubated during teenage years and matured by the time I entered college. There have been many friends that followed, but it was through Fred that I first realized what is unique about a true friend—the ability to see the value within.

Fred and I attended a large boys' public high school in Brooklyn and we both commuted from our homes to school by subway. We often met by chance in the front of the first subway car in the late afternoon after school was over. Summers in New York City were hot and the subways were even hotter. The tunnels were filled with the stale air that multiplied overnight beneath the city. But we seemed to have found a helpful solution to the heat. The front of the train had a single window that could be opened as the subway hurtled through the dark tunnels, creating a breeze that provided some relief from the heat, although not from the accumulated soot. It was there in that unlikely situation that Fred and I first explored what was to become a true friendship.

Fred was serious and gentle. He had large rimmed glasses that seemed to advertise his intellectual capacity. The high school that we attended was intensely academic and focused on providing advanced education. We challenged one another with what we were learning in a broad range of topics.

I'm not certain how many times we met before he asked me an unusual and seemingly inappropriate question: "Do you know what 'born again' means?"

I was momentarily startled but not offended. It was the first time he asked about anything that had to do with religion or spiritual issues. I recalled having read something about being "born again" in the New Testament. Religion was not new to me as I had been formally confirmed in a German Lutheran church where, under the stern tutelage of Pastor Kropp, I had memorized Luther's catechism in German and recited back portions to the congregation on confirmation day. But perhaps it was the directness of Fred's question that startled me into thinking about its meaning. He continued, explaining the story of Nicodemus and his secretive late-night meeting with Jesus.

I believe that Fred was wise enough and knew me well enough to realize that his question would provoke me into a quest to try to understand its meaning. Over the years that followed I returned to the story over and over again and wondered why Fred had chosen to ask me the question about being born again. As we became closer friends, Fred continued to talk to me about spiritual matters. I realized the answer to the question of why Fred chose me was because he saw something in me that even I did not understand. For the first time I realized that here was someone who saw in me sufficient value to risk talking about my spiritual well-being.

During the remaining years in high school we became close friends. Fred was an encourager. Looking back, I now see that he was carefully guiding me in my newly awakened spiritual journey. He was instilling in me a sense of personal value and it was a wonderful gift from him. Fred was materially poor but the gift that he had given me was of great value and one that would endure.

Fred was unembarrassed about where he lived and the circumstances of his life. When I visited him in his home above a nondescript storefront in the Flatbush section of Brooklyn, we climbed up two flights of stairs and entered an apartment through the kitchen. It was unnecessary to go further. From that vantage point you could see the entire apartment—the living room that also served as a bedroom and the dining room. I wondered where he studied at night. Fred lived alone with his mother. His father, a chronic alcoholic, had disappeared when he was young. I was stricken by this person who had so little of material goods yet was able to share so much more through his spiritual beliefs, something that he seemed to have in abundance.

Fred and I remained friends throughout high school. He mentored me through many of my feelings of inadequacy. Although I had loving and caring parents, as immigrants in a strange country they had difficulty in imparting to me the self-confidence that I could succeed in my education. Fred saw my potential and walked me through the highly competitive and difficult classes in our high school. During times of discouragement he was always there. He truly cared for and understood me as he helped me in my early spiritual journey. He gently encouraged me, a shy young boy, to participate with him in the activities of our school and his church group. It was through these experiences that I gained the confidence to reach out beyond the shelter of my inner person to enter into life experiences that encompassed my entire being.

Fred and I lost contact when I went away to college and subsequently to medical school. I continued my education and training in medicine. Fred and his family moved to California when he accepted a position as a physicist in a private company. When I later moved to California with my family we merely crossed paths as "ships in the night." Fred was returning to the East coast to accept a teaching position at a Quaker school in Pennsylvania. Fred's new position seemed to be well suited to what he was so good at—teaching and mentoring high school students, and no doubt selecting individuals of value and challenging them to reach their full potential.

Over the years Fred did not leave my memory. I interpreted his boldness in asking "Do you know what 'born again' means?" to mean that I was of value. It initiated an inner quest to find deeper spiritual value in my life. Fred was a friend in a moment of time but a friendship that endured in my memory. It is for all that he did for me, even though it was only during a brief time in my early life, that I realize how great a value he was as a friend.

AN UNLIKELY PRISON FRIENDSHIP

As our conversation progresses, we realize that we both have had experiences that parallel the story of Paul and Onesimus. We see that friendships may not always occur as a consequence of deliberate cultivation. They can in fact occur under unexpected circumstances. We take another look at Paul's letter to see how this applies.

In Paul's letter to Philemon about Onesimus, he suggests that they were strangers destined to minister to one another in prison. Onesimus provided for Paul's physical needs and, in turn, Paul met the spiritual and emotional needs of Onesimus by providing him with the forgiveness and friendship that were desperately needed by the runaway slave. During the time that they were together, their friendship evolved into a deeper spiritual relationship. It was a friendship that began with the Paul's recognition of value within Onesimus. He was no longer an obscure, invisible slave. He had become the valued son Paul never had.

FOR SUCH A TIME AS THIS

While many of us may think that friendships are for a lifetime, there may be brief deep friendships that arise from special circumstances, often unanticipated and often unplanned, that are for only a limited time in one's life. In a way, they emerge as something of a mystery because they come at a time of unique or special personal needs. Even those who are already surrounded by friends may experience the unexpected discovery of a new and unique friend. Early in the relationship these friendships may evoke questions as to "Why now?" or "For what purpose?" Eventually the questions are answered. Perhaps it is to bring two people together to find deeper meaning in both of their lives. Perhaps during a period of depression, an illness, or loneliness a new friend is embraced who meets a special need or brings strength, vision, or spiritual transformation. But whatever the reason, the value of the person must first be recognized. Only then will the personal relationship of friendship follow.

We compare specific friendships developed during times of difficult circumstances—a tragic death, a diagnosis of cancer, a job loss, or an emotionally overwhelming period within life itself. We conclude that God arranges for us to meet these new friends. They are not chance encounters.

God knows the value of a person and he knows each one's journey. At one point he may bring two people together at an intersection of need. We may view the meeting as random but God maintains a resource of people with special gifts that he specifically directs toward us at a crucial moment. These are people who see value in others. It is as if he gathers a host of pre-identified individuals and selects the one who, in time of need, is able to come alongside us and transform our lives. These friends are gifts from God.

What is so wonderful about these friends is that they seem so perfect for the moment. They appear to have been designed for our very own need, whether it is emotional, spiritual, or physical. A disquieting difficulty comes when they may be with us for only for a moment in time and then we must let go of them no matter how strongly we feel the need for that friendship. Paul acknowledged the value of Onesimus to himself, but was very much aware of how even he had to let go of a friend, even one of such great value. We come to see that Paul's principle applies to us; we may need to relinquish a friend who can also be of significant value to another.

Another dimension is opened as we realize that the letter of Paul to Philemon acknowledges that in our lifelong need for friends there are no age limitations or barriers. The elderly, who are more likely to have lost a brother, sister, father, mother, wife or husband, are just as in need of friendship as a young child—perhaps more so. They wrestle with the sense of abandonment and the perception that they are no longer of value. They worry that they are becoming invisible. New friends meet vital emotional and spirituals needs. The elderly, who feel increasingly isolated and lonely, need the friendship of others, even a younger person, to convey the message, "We still see value in you for who you are." This was the case with Onesimus and Paul.

> Yet I appeal to you on the basis of love. I then, as Paul—an old man and now also a prisoner of Christ Jesus—I appeal to you for my son Onesimus, who became my son while I was in chains. Formerly he was useless to you, but now he has become useful both to you and to me. I am sending him—who is my very heart—back to you. I would have liked to keep him with me so that he could take your place in helping me while I am in chains for the gospel.
>
> (Phlm 9–13)

Again we compare our own life stories and find that we each have experienced a close friendship for a season, but became confused and saddened when the friendship ended abruptly. Even as parents must eventually let go of their children, friends may need to release one another, no matter how much value they see in each other, and how much it hurts to let go. In God's plan, our friendships are not solely for our benefit, but also for others who need someone who will bring hope. In spite of his feelings, Paul realized that Onesimus was "his" for only a period of time.

There are circumstances when friendships fade—not because of some event that threatens the friendship or because the friendship is superseded by another or because the person is no longer viewed as valuable. Sometimes gradual changes occur in individual lives over time as each person matures, interests change, families intervene, occupations interfere, needs diverge, and mutual support is no longer needed. It would be wrong, however, to dismiss past friends as somehow no longer of value in our lifelong journey. A friendship, once formed, prepares us for the next level of intimacy that takes us deeper into seeing the value in others. They are forever integrated as part of our history.

JESUS' EXTREME EXAMPLE

Friendships are not to be taken lightly. Few of us have encountered circumstances that require us to consider what Jesus taught when he said, "My command is this: Love each other as I have loved you. Greater love has no one than this: to lay down one's life for one's friends" (John 15:12–13)

As the conversation about friends progresses, Arthur confesses that one of his great challenges with Scripture is trying to understand the teaching of Jesus that says we must be willing to give up our own lives for our friends. We discuss the weighty question, "How literally are we to interpret what Jesus meant in his teaching on love, obedience, and friends?"

It certainly has to do with how deeply we value the person whom we call our friend. When Jesus said, "Greater love has no one than this: to lay down one's life for one's friends" (John 15:13), did that include his life and journey only, or ours as well? We are told later in the Scriptures that indeed we are included. "This is how we know what love is: Jesus Christ laid down his life for us. And we ought to lay down our lives for our brothers and sisters" (1 John 3:16).

This is a shocking, almost frightening conclusion about the value of friends—a conclusion that perhaps we may hope refers only to the life and death of Jesus and not to ourselves. Our fear may be that one day we may be called on to do this—die for a friend. But the importance of friendship lies in just this extreme. Jesus did not say love is to give up your life for a dream or a cause or a country, but for a friend. This is how deeply he defined love, by seeing value in a friend. I heard Arthur speak of his travels to the violent regions of the eastern Democratic Republic of Congo where he has seen just this—friends giving up their life to save that of another—often a defenseless woman or child.

There is circularity in the teaching of Jesus on love, obedience, and deep friendship. What is clear is that he was committed to these principles, as shown by his own life and death for his friends. His obedience to God was absolute, and his commitment and love included his own death. What lay behind his death was not a spirit of martyrdom but the value he saw in all people.

We wonder how far we may be willing to go for a friend. Few if any of us will be called on to give up our life, but we may be required to lay down a part of our life to demonstrate our love for a friend. So we ask ourselves the question, "What part of our life would we be willing to sacrifice or lay down for the sake of a real friend?" Is this simply a metaphor, and is it so extreme to our ears that we allow ourselves the option of summarily dismissing a need to respond? When we auger in on these hard words of Jesus, we might turn and ask him, "What do you mean, Lord? What would you have me sacrifice for this friend?" We may find a myriad of possibilities cascading into sight. It may be in the form of time, energy, changing our own plans or opinion—or as ordinary as listening to a heart as well as words, going for a walk, or sharing a meal. Few of us will be called on to step into harm's way to save a child, donate a kidney, or be a bone marrow donor, but then again, perhaps we might. Are we ready for any of the above?

THINK ON THESE THINGS

1. Who have been important friends in your life experience? What traits set them apart from all the others?

2. How did a friend become "visible" to you? What value did you discover in them?

3. What do you think Jesus meant when he said, "Greater love has no one than this: to lay down one's life for one's friends" (John 15:13). How far would you go for a friend? How far has a friend gone for you?

4. Have you experienced transformation within friendship? Has it been mutual?

2

Value between Brothers and Sisters

Perhaps the reason he was separated from you for a little while was that you might have him back forever—no longer as a slave, but better than a slave, as a dear brother. He is very dear to me but even dearer to you, both as a fellow man and as a brother in the Lord. / Your love has given me great joy and encouragement, because you, brother, have refreshed the hearts of the Lord's people. (Phlm 15–16, 7)

Fortified with our second cup of coffee, we linger around the table recalling tales of childhood adventures with our own siblings. The conversation eventually turns from stories of mischief and pranks to recognition of the real impact and significant influence of siblings in our lives.

Soon Arthur ties the conversation back to meaning drawn from the intertwined relationships of Paul, Onesimus, and Philemon. Paul's intervention between slave and master reveals an unusual turn for that day and that culture. Little affection passed between master and slave, and in fact little notice was extended to one of such low estate as Onesimus by a man of the stature and position as Philemon. It was as if Onesimus, although living and working in the home of Philemon, were invisible.

Paul returned Onesimus to Philemon no longer as a slave but as a brother. The relationship implies a stronger bond than mere friendship. The difference between brothers and sisters as compared to friendships is that the former are biological relationships that can only be partially severed. Friendships can be dissolved instantaneously and just as quickly restored. Little children recognize this when they shout, "You will never be my friend again!" and then, the very next day, behave as though nothing had happened.

There are heartrending stories about relationships between brothers and sisters. Although linked together by genetic bonds and years of common experiences, they may separate deliberately with only occasional meetings and rare communication. Even hatred may develop between brothers and sisters. Throughout history the bitter story of Cain and Able has been told to illustrate just how severely broken a relationship can become. Many literary plots are based upon this very event. Some salient examples come to mind.

FRACTURED RELATIONSHIPS

The Brothers Karamazov, Dostoyevsky's 1880 novel, is a tale of brothers steeped in rivalry, misdirected love, rage, and death. We also see the Japanese filmmaker Akira Kurosawa, in his epic film *Ran*, a Japanese version of *King Lear*, as he portrays three brothers who are intent on destroying one another and the kingdom over which their father rules. The father becomes a broken and despondent man. When challenged as to why God allows such death and destruction, the father looks up to the sky and asks, "When did God tell you to make swords and weapons to kill each other?" Then there is the American writer John Steinbeck, in his novel *East of Eden*, in reference to the biblical land of Nod, to which Cain fled. He extracts the tension between two brothers who struggle for their father's love in a classic "Cain and Abel" setting. The Old Testament story of Joseph describes a setting of envy and deceit, but in this instance it does not end with the tragic outcome woven into so many of the stories of conflict between brothers and sisters. Instead, it ends with forgiveness initiated by Joseph, the one who was harmed the most, who must have spent years in deep despondency wrestling with how he could have been viewed as having so little value as to be sold by his brothers. Nevertheless, he saw value in his brothers, which made reconciliation possible.

These are stories of brothers who are entwined in jealousy, hatred, and a search for love and acceptance. They span all cultures throughout the world. Yet Paul uses the phrase "brothers and sisters in Christ" to describe the closeness of Christian fellowship. It is consistent with the concept of the family of God—God the Father, Jesus the Son, the children of God as brothers and sisters—all bound by a spiritual union. It is not surprising therefore that the value of sibling relationships may reach far beyond that of many others. There is a spiritual dimension of belonging that may be intimate, enduring, and lasting.

The account of Joseph and his brothers is worthy of review.

> Then Joseph could no longer control himself before all his attendants, and he cried out, "Have everyone leave my presence!" So there was no one with Joseph when he made himself known to his brothers. And he wept so loudly that the Egyptians heard him, and Pharaoh's household heard about it.
>
> Joseph said to his brothers, "I am Joseph! Is my father still living?" But his brothers were not able to answer him, because they were terrified at his presence.
>
> Then Joseph said to his brothers, "Come close to me." When they had done so, he said, "I am your brother Joseph, the one you sold into Egypt! And now, do not be distressed and do not be angry with yourselves for selling me here, because it was to save lives that God sent me ahead of you. (Gen 45:1–5)

Brothers and sisters are brought into this world not through chance, but by the very design of God. No matter how stressful, difficult, or threatening these relationships may be, it is crucial for brothers and sisters to see the value in one another and for each to acknowledge the opportunity to return the other to God as better for having been with one another.

Our conversation once again turns very personal. As Arthur tells the story of his sister, he is unable to finish without tears coming to his eyes as he recalls how valuable their relationship had been in spite of her desperate circumstances.

THE STORY OF MILDRED

My sister was mentally ill almost all of her life. When it became obvious, it was diagnosed as paranoid schizophrenia. My parents and relatives, all immigrants from Germany who believed in a strong work ethic, concluded that her cure should be harder work, abundant food, and liberal doses of sunshine.

Mildred was brilliant. I, the younger brother, unfortunately always followed her by one year in school and suffered embarrassing comparisons to her. Teachers would say, "Why aren't you as smart as your sister?" The words pained me deeply and did not motivate me to do my best. Nevertheless, they never interfered with my relationship with my sister and I always held her in high esteem.

Her illness first appeared in late high school. She began to withdraw socially and held on to only one or two of her closest friends. The simplest explanation in our Germanic culture was that she was an introvert who loved to read and was uncomfortable in crowds.

When I went away to college and subsequently to medical school, I had only brief contact with her, mostly on holidays and short vacations. My mother always reported that all was well and never relayed any information that could be construed as negative, especially if it had anything to do with mental illness. She reported that my sister was working as a secretary, earning a good salary, and investing her money faithfully while living at home. She was unaware that none of it was true.

During my first year of marriage and my third year of medical school, my mother called in tears. They had discovered that my sister had not been working for over three years. In the overly protective environment of my Germanic family, she was able to live and eat at home in economic security. Each day, my mother made lunch for her to take to work, and each day gave her spending money, telling her to save her earnings. My father, a gentle and kind man who worked long hard days in a bakery, did not have the time or inclination to probe beyond what my mother would tell him.

Although my parents were in pain, I cannot imagine the pain my sister must have been in. For three years she left home each morning, found somewhere to "live" during the day, and retreated home in the evening to recount a life that did not exist. During the day she traveled in subways and lived in museums, public libraries, and movie theaters.

Mildred was always well dressed. The unpaid bills that began to accumulate indicated that she shopped in expensive stores. Undoubtedly, it was the unpaid bills that precipitated the crisis, especially in a family where frugality meant never borrowing and always paying in cash.

She must have had a fearful existence as the schizophrenia enveloped her mind. Her writings and poems, initially beautiful and intellectual, became more detailed, and soon emulated the tangled writings of Virginia Woolf's *Mrs. Dalloway*, evolving into an assemblage of words separated by semicolons. Eventually they became random and confused and reflected obvious paranoia. Throughout her writings were traces of Søren Kierkegaard's *Fear and Trembling*. Her seemingly disjointed writings were a quest to find spiritual answers for a confused mind.

Over a period of years her disease progressed. The paranoia became more severe and as a result she alienated most of our relatives. My parents continued to have simple solutions that were meant to evoke miracles—a trip, a move to a new location, a new nutrient or vitamin in mega-doses. Eventually it all came crashing in. The violence became too threatening. I, especially, became the target of her paranoia. Her outrage and accusations became more frightening and as a family, with the exception of my sister, we reached a difficult decision—institutionalization and electric shock therapy.

In the 1960s there were no drugs that really worked for psychiatric disorders and no easy solutions. As a medical student, I had minimal knowledge of psychiatric disorders or of the benefit and risks of electric shock therapy, and so I consented, along with my parents, to a draconian procedure that may or may not help.

After the terrible electrocution of her brain was completed, I sat in front of her in silence filled with fear of the consequences of our decision. The paranoia was gone but so was any semblance of her intellect. What remained was basic, childlike communication. Where had all those good memories gone? How much of her intellect was permanently erased? Were the beautiful thoughts vaporized along with the paranoia? The person before me was not the person with whom I had shared childhood memories and joys. I likened her to a cocoon and butterfly and hoped for the beauty of a resurrection. I hoped and prayed that she would emerge as herself without the ghost of mental illness to haunt her.

Over the decades that followed we went from good years to bad and back to good again. Sometimes it was so painful I wanted to walk away. I had my own family, a wife and children, and they needed my attention as well.

As new drugs became available for mental disorders, we found that they could control the paranoia for varying periods of time but always at some expense to her mind. Often we would sit and talk within the shadow of her mental illness. I longed for her to once again create those wonderful poems and delve into the intellectual writings that she had produced and I enjoyed. I wanted to look into her face and see what had brought us to a close relationship as young children—not a face draped in depression.

Unable to work, my sister continued to live at home. My parents cared for her until it came time in their old age for her to care for them. But by this time she was a mere child, insulated from real-world experiences and responsibilities. My wife and I had to make major decisions for her. We took take care of the rent, the bills, the daily issues of living as well as her increasing health problems. The side effects of the drugs that subdued her illness eroded both her body and mind.

I could always tell when she was going to become severely paranoid again. It was preceded by a brief time when she seemed to "wake up" as if she had been a "sleeping beauty." She was conversational, engaging, and energetic and took on challenges—there was a resurrection of her intellect. As she improved she would begin skipping her daily medication and soon her paranoia would return, coupled with the most amazing memory of the past, as if to say to all of us, "See, it was not all destroyed with those bolts of electricity that ripped through my brain."

My sister died at age sixty-five. The last two years were remarkable. Both my parents died in their eighties, after which she lived alone. In addition to schizophrenia, she had developed asthma, required steroids, and as a result became severely osteoporotic. The osteoporosis resulted in fractured vertebra, which further complicated her care. Often we would have to employ caregivers to help her physically maneuver around the house that we rented for her. But she never complained about her illnesses, the chronic pain, or her past suffering and she never ever let us know about her terrible depression. Throughout it all, the ups and downs, the screaming, the threats of violence, I never lost the essence of her value as a sister who came out so strongly when she was well.

In retrospect I realized a transformation had occurred in my sister with the birth of our granddaughter Sophia. There was a bond between them that was difficult to explain. All of us observed it. When she held our little granddaughter in her arms, swaddled as if she were a special treasure, her entire face was a smile of radiant peace. I read in her expression, "See, here I am holding this baby girl and I am content at last. I am of value to this infant." Sometimes I feel that Mildred was so very close to God during her illness that she had asked him to provide a special blessing to both of them—she and Sophia.

I would not dare to interpret the meaning of her transformation. Perhaps it was always a dream of hers to hold what she could never have. Perhaps she saw the innocence of that baby as the same innocence she once possessed before the mental illness descended on her.

Her wonderful new health lasted for an additional year. Then she became terribly ill physically and required hospitalization, intubation, and artificial life support. Because we had feared this might happen, we had discussed what she wanted us to do under these circumstances. After several days of intubation it was clear that she would not improve. Communicating by means of written notes, we agreed to stop the ventilation so that she could talk freely with each one of us and say a final farewell after the many years of suffering.

We prayed in the intensive care unit of the hospital. She clutched my hand tightly as she slowly slipped into a coma. A peace enveloped both of us. I stayed with her until she breathed her last, continuing to hold her hand as it grew colder. I could not hold back the tears. As she looked at me with that same aura of contentment, her last words were, "Don't cry for me, Arthur."

The story of my sister is neither happy nor sad. It is some of both, and near the end of her life she at last enjoyed one of her happiest periods. It is not for me to determine when and if she saw her life as having value in spite of her severe disabilities. But in that brief moment, when she held our granddaughter Sophia in her arms and smiled with holy contentment, I sensed for at least a brief moment that she felt she was of value in a new creation.

After a hushed moment, Arthur tells how they deeply missed his sister. How years of pain and suffering came to a peaceful close but not before she experienced a type of rebirth. As he reflected on that last year, he realized that they were given a gift of one of the happiest years she ever had. They returned her to God, no longer to suffer a life of mental distortions, but as an individual, free at last from the suffocating depression that held her captive for most of her life. When we see value in a person much can be endured. Arthur finishes the story.

There were many opportunities during my sister's years of paranoia to sever our relationship. At times she was verbally violent and occasionally physically abusive as well. Many times I feared for the safety of my parents or my wife and children. The stress of caring for her and our parents, who were paralyzed by their lack of understanding of mental illness, seemed overwhelming at times. Often I just wanted to walk away to some peaceful place.

The shared lifetime experiences of brothers and sisters are a potent force to bring value to relationships regardless of what transpires in future years. Whether disagreements, illnesses, or other divisions occur, those who have had a strong loving relationship must do all that they can do to preserve it. Those who have been wounded or discouraged by a brother or sister relationship must hope and pray for restoration. Lives are too precious to discard over petty disagreements or even severe mental illness.

BARBARA'S BROTHER

Arthur's story about Mildred touched me in a deep way. I realize it is because my shaky relationship with my own brother came cascading back to my mind. We were so entirely different in nature that even as small children we were almost invisible to each other. I was outgoing, made friends easily, and loved school and studies. He was a loner, shy, loved dogs, had few friends, and struggled with school. As adults, we drifted farther apart as he moved to the West Coast from Chicago and experienced several difficult marriages. We had enjoyable though infrequent visits through the years, just enough to be assured that we had mutual love and interest in each other even with so little contact. He had cast off the faith of our church upbringing until an unexpected turn changed everything.

He was diagnosed with an aggressive brain tumor at the age of sixty-four, and several months later he died. There was one day, however, that brought us back together, and brought the glorious promise of spending eternity together. Through a gentle nurse who cared deeply, he rejected his years of proclaimed atheism and embraced his childhood faith in Jesus, the one we both had heard of at the knee of our great-grandmother. During our last visit, when he could no longer form words, we tearfully shared in the knowledge that we loved each other and would spend a heavenly eternity together. He was now clearly visible and clearly peaceful, a transforming gift for both of us.

The transformation of Onesimus gives us an example of hope that a fractured relationship, regardless of the cause, can be restored. The Old Testament story of Joseph and his brothers informs us that forgiveness between brothers and sisters is always possible even though years pass and wounds are deep. We are never to be in the position of giving up, always viewing our brother or sister as a divine original—an individual of value.

THINK ON THESE THINGS

1. What is your best memory of a sibling? How long has it been since you spent relational time with them?

2. What are promoters and detractors to positive sibling relationships?

3. What effects do rifts between siblings have on entire families and beyond? What do you think can be done to repair and/or prevent such disagreements?

4. Whether or not you have siblings, do you have anyone in your life who became like a brother or sister? What brought you to that point?

3

Value within Generations

It is as none other than Paul—an old man and now also a prisoner of Christ Jesus—that I appeal to you for my son Onesimus, who became my son while I was in chains. Formerly he was useless to you, but now he has become useful both to you and to me. I am sending him—who is my very heart—back to you. (Phlm 9b–12)

I lean in to listen to Arthur, and it suddenly dawns on me who he really is and what he brings to the subject of children. As a pediatrician, he has interacted with them throughout his long career. I tune in with keen ears and utmost attention. This man knows children! He knows them inside and out—he has seen parents at their best and worst. His heart still melts with compassion when he sees a child suffer, be abused or misunderstood. Now he weaves together a tapestry of remarkable stories and principles that once again underscore emerging truths from Paul's letter to Philemon. We see the process of discovery within intimate family relationships as a two-way street—children and their elders, learning about and learning from each other—coming out the other side with a new sense of value for one another.

Our discussion begins with our own experiences. Arthur makes the observation that inevitably, during conversations with friends, childhood experiences become a topic of discussion. He explains how often he is surprised to find himself as one of few individuals who looks back and remembers his childhood with happiness and gratefulness.

ARTHUR'S CHILDHOOD MEMORIES

I was nurtured in an environment of love. There's nothing I would change—not even the episodes of discipline when my mother chased me around the dining room table, wooden spoon in hand, threatening to use it if I did not go to my room immediately. The discipline was meant to correct my stubbornness or the transgressions that with time became learning experiences in a boyhood that was rich in security and love.

On the surface, my childhood may not seem ideal to others. I was born into a poor immigrant family, lived on a dead-end street (not a cul-de-sac), and was just one house removed from the railroad tracks. I had to walk from the "wrong" neighborhood across the railroad tracks to go to public school, learning early in childhood the meaning of the "wrong side of the tracks." It was only when I left Brooklyn and went to Wheaton College in midwestern Illinois that I realized how little our family had in material possessions. However, surrounded by love and security, I never thought of myself as poor.

I realized how hard my parents worked and how little they demanded for themselves. My father was a baker, and often worked long hours into the night, seven days a week, especially before holidays, when the demands for baked goods increased dramatically. My mother nurtured my sister and me in a gentle and indulgent European manner, providing us with good food and developing holiday traditions around family and relatives. She made certain that we took advantage of the many benefits of living in New York City—parks, museums, botanical gardens, summers at the beach, swimming in the ocean, all accessible by means of a five-cent ride on public transportation and a lunch in a brown bag. Growing up, I felt very secure indeed. The world around me belonged to me and it seemed good.

My parents also laid the foundation for my spiritual journey. We were taken to Sunday school and church. It was not a simple process as we traveled through Brooklyn by subway to a distant German Lutheran Church. There I memorized my way through Luther's catechism under the stern tutelage of Pastor Kropp. Although it was a foundation in orthodox religion, it was formal and primarily intellectual, without deep spiritual content. Nevertheless it was a foundation to build on.

We talk about parental security, love, and spiritual strength being the foundational pillars allowing children to mature and step out with confidence into an often hostile world. We also observe that it is often difficult for parents to let go, even of grown children who should be independent. A striking example of tough love and parenting is found in a famous Bible parable about the "Prodigal Son."

Yes, at times parents may find it difficult to release their children to an unknown destiny. "Letting go" may threaten several decades of nurturing and protection and they may do all that they can to keep a child close. Carried to an extreme, these same factors may be harmful. The story of the wayward son in the Gospel of Luke is a story that some of us may fear because we are never certain that our ending will be the safe return of our child who we value so highly that we are reluctant to let go. This graphic parable told by Jesus presents much fodder for thinking of parent-child relationships.

WHEN CHILDREN WANDER

Jesus continued: "There was a man who had two sons. The younger one said to his father, 'Father, give me my share of the estate.' So he divided his property between them.

"Not long after that, the younger son got together all he had, set off for a distant country and there squandered his wealth in wild living. After he had spent everything, there was a severe famine in that whole country, and he began to be in need. So he went and hired himself out to a citizen of that country, who sent him to his fields to feed pigs. He longed to fill his stomach with the pods that the pigs were eating, but no one gave him anything.

"When he came to his senses, he said, 'How many of my father's hired servants have food to spare, and here I am starving to death! I will set out and go back to my father and say to him: Father, I have sinned against heaven and against you. I am no longer worthy to be called your son; make me like one of your hired servants.' So he got up and went to his father.

"But while he was still a long way off, his father saw him and was filled with compassion for him; he ran to his son, threw his arms around him and kissed him.

"The son said to him, 'Father, I have sinned against heaven and against you. I am no longer worthy to be called your son.'

"But the father said to his servants, 'Quick! Bring the best robe and put it on him. Put a ring on his finger and sandals on his feet. Bring the fattened calf and kill it. Let's have a feast and celebrate. For this son of mine was dead and is alive again; he was lost and is found.' So they began to celebrate." (Luke 15:11–24)

We are not given every detail of the story of the lost son—only enough perhaps to apply it to some aspect of our own experience. The ingredients are critical—a loving parent who provides for his children, and a son who in spite of love and care, seems to reject everything that was done for him, turns away, and leaves it all behind. Perhaps the father knew all too well what might happen, but we must believe that he had both the hope and faith that one day he would again embrace his son with compassion, love, and forgiveness. Though not physically present, the wayward son remained visible to the father, allowing him to respond with joy and forgiveness on seeing him return.

There are lessons from the story of the wayward son—to always remember the value in a relationship and to love, provide security, and forgive our children even when they seemingly abandon the love and security that we provide and when we have been wounded as parents. This is an image of God. It is the way he views us and it is the way we are to view our own children because each child, no matter how wayward, is of great value.

As we return to the story of Onesimus, we see a fresh perspective. It is a story of someone who was ignored and not valued, who by leaving, connected with another individual who could see the inherent value in him and cause transformation. This leads us into further observations of family dynamics today.

The way in which we, and the society in which we live, view our children is critical to how we act toward them and whether they will be transformed into the persons that God has destined them to be. Children are not optional appendages to "round out" a family. They are treasures on loan from God. As the letter to Philemon illustrates, they are individuals of great value to be returned "better" for having been with us. They may leave us but they are always in God's possession.

Children must be viewed as our future and taught to preserve the good in the world. We must not inadvertently become co-conspirators in the perpetuation of that which is evil or destructive. Without the loving and caring influence of parents and grandparents, there are far too many nefarious individuals willing to step into a void and catapult an unsuspecting child in the wrong direction. We read these strong admonitions from the pages of the Old Testament.

> Only be careful, and watch yourselves closely so that you do not forget the things your eyes have seen or let them fade from your heart as long as you live. Teach them to your children and to their children after them. Remember the day you stood before the LORD your God at Horeb, when he said to me, "Assemble the people before me to hear my words so that they may learn to revere me as long as they live in the land and may teach them to their children. (Deut 4:9–10)

> Fix these words of mine in your hearts and minds; tie them as symbols on your hands and bind them on your foreheads. Teach them to your children, talking about them when you sit at home and when you walk along the road, when you lie down and when you get up. Write them on the doorframes of your houses and on your gates, so that your days and the days of your children may be many in the land the LORD swore to give your ancestors, as many as the days that the heavens are above the earth. (Deut 11:18–21)

The story of Onesimus reveals that a person (who might be a child) can become physically invisible for a period of time, as was the case when he ran away from Philemon. It may be under circumstances, as in the story of the wayward son, that are deeply troubling or even frightening. Yet God is with them during that time, somehow walking before them, preserving and protecting them, even when they reach the point of complete want and desperation.

We realize how often children actually leave home under trying circumstances. I wonder how often they come under a positive influence and return with new perspective.

No matter how spiritual we consider ourselves, or how much we pray for our children, or how we devote ourselves to them, it is often the case that their true value and their spiritual transformation takes place under another's guidance—a friend, a pastor, a youth minister, even an encounter with a stranger in a time away from home. It is crucial for us to be open to God's ways even when those ways are painful.

It was in prison that the value of Onesimus became visible to Paul through a mutual life-transforming encounter. In the case of the wayward son, he journeyed into desperation and destitution. We would not have planned either of these scenarios as the hope is to avoid them, or at a minimum experience them on our own terms or timelines.

In the story of the wayward son, God had important lessons for both the father and son to learn. For the son, it was that he could go home to a father who remained steadfast and forgiving and who valued him unconditionally in spite of all that happened. The father learned that he had not lost the capacity to love and forgive a son who had abandoned all the love and security he had provided. It would have been only too easy to say, "So, you have come back home only after you lost everything and there is no place else to go," or to scold, "I told you this would happen. You have wasted all the hard earned money that I entrusted to you."

ROLE REVERSALS

Another aspect of family life emerges as we explore a curious phenomenon of child-adult role reversal. Arthur's wisdom testifies to this through his many experiences with child-parent interaction over the years.

The way in which we view our role as parents has a lot to do with how we view our children's role in the family. As adults, we often make the assumption that we are the sole teachers, providing our children with knowledge and wisdom to journey through life. We may say, "Teachers teach students; students don't teach teachers," or in the case of a pediatrician like myself, "We help children in their illnesses; they don't help us," or in the case of parents, "Parents teach children; children don't teach parents." In all these relationships there is an assumption that the role of the adult is to help, instruct, and care for the child—or so it may seem. If we assume this is a one-way process, we are wrong. If we are not learning from our children, we are not listening to them.

> And he said: "I tell you the truth, unless you change and become like little children, you will never enter the kingdom of heaven. Therefore, whoever takes the lowly position like this child is the greatest in the kingdom of heaven." (Matt 18:3–4)

Although our two families hardly knew each other during our child-rearing years, we find that we have much in common in our ways of parenting and grand parenting. We both delight in the fact that as grandparents we become an added bonus in many respects, with opportunities to nurture, amplifying our contributions with a perspective tempered by age. Often it is a grandparent who has the ability to truly connect with a child. Grandparents are extra special because of their ability to listen carefully and patiently without passing judgment. Grandparents, perhaps more than parents, are keen listeners to children. They often are aware of the importance of a young child's influence in an adult's life, and acknowledge both the happiness and the value that has entered their life through a grandchild.

Grandchildren seem to understand that most grandparents see their value in the current moment, not for what they will become, or what others might want them to become. Grandparents have time to laugh at stories, and tell stories—to immerse themselves in sadness and to listen to concerns while remaining neutral in their opinions. For many grandchildren, their grandparents are the repository of the history of their parents, who alone can convey what they were like as children, how they behaved (or misbehaved), and the struggles that brought them to adulthood, ever learning and ever hopeful.

A child can change our life and impart deep meaning for a parent or grandparent. Jesus knew that a child could transmit knowledge to an adult and he also knew that a child could bring a relationship of value to adults. Arthur experienced this with a child named Mark, a patient who helped him understand death and human frailty—his own as well as that of others.

MARK'S STORY

I remember a phone call from a referring pediatrician. He had a new patient with recurrent infections who had a lengthy family history of five deaths among male cousins—all from infection—all before one year of age. I knew almost immediately that the most likely diagnosis was that of an inherited disease called "severe combined immunodeficiency." The disease is so named because both the antibody and the cellular immune systems are severely deficient. Without the protection conferred by both systems, infants are susceptible to lethal infections from viruses, bacteria, and fungi and rarely live for more than a year.

After Mark arrived at the hospital we obtained a routine blood count and a chest x-ray to look for a thymus gland. The thymus is a gland that produces cells for the immune system and is located just beneath the breastbone in front of the heart. Both tests supported our initial diagnosis—the white blood cell count was low and the thymus could not be visualized. Additional studies showed that Mark had no immunity. Mark would ultimately die from some overwhelming infection just as his cousins did, unless he received treatment.

There were difficult decisions confronting the family and the medical staff. At that time there was no standard treatment. What was offered was an experimental transplant, which might work or result in a potentially fatal outcome. Thus we embarked on a journey with Mark and his family that was to include the uncertainties of experimental treatment.

We performed a transplant and waited for evidence that Mark's immune system was working. But weeks passed slowly and it was months before we had objective evidence that his immune system was recovering. Mark was sent home with some optimism but also with an uncertain future.

Soon the transplant showed signs of working and Mark was amazingly healthy for four years. He was a normal child, free from infections, and could come and go as he pleased, mingling with relatives and other children, without contracting any serious infections. As we followed Mark during routine visits to our clinics, I began to sense that there was something special about this child. Initially it was hard to pinpoint, but this was a four-year-old child who seemed to listen to and understand every word that I spoke to him and his parents. Often he looked at me, and those that surrounded him, as if he understood our inner thoughts.

I am not certain exactly when Mark's health began to deteriorate, but it was gradual in his fourth year of life. His immune function showed signs of deteriorating on one of the many tests that we routinely performed. Shortly after the family returned from a vacation in Arizona, they brought Mark to me. He was severely dehydrated from diarrhea, which had started in Arizona and continued for a week after their return.

Mark was difficult to take care of during the last year of his life—not because of Mark, but because of Brian, his father, and his anger. Some of it was understandable as there was little he could do to make his son healthy again. But it made Mark's care extremely difficult and frequently alienated the very people that Mark needed most for his healthcare—nurses, interns, and residents who became reluctant to deal with Brian and who were fearful of his unpredictable outbursts.

I felt that, in spite of his young age of four years, Mark knew what was happening. Without our speaking the words, he understood what we were beginning to feel—that he would not get better and that he might soon die. During the next months Mark needed his father to understand, but Brian's anger made it difficult for his own son to live and perhaps to die well. In a way, I was wrong. Brian made it difficult for himself. Mark was accepting his own death and helping others, as well as his father, to accept his death. Indeed, as time passed we all learned that this four-year-old child was to become our teacher and, remarkably, he began a process of teaching his adult caretakers how to compassionately care for a sick and dying child, and ultimately how to accept death itself.

Mark took me on a spiritual journey. He looked on his own pain and suffering with uncanny spiritual insight and found reasons why he was better off than others. Mark needed frequent injections of antibiotics and blood tests. It was always difficult to start the IVs, which sometimes took hours of poking through the skin before an adequate vein was found. After one of these particularly traumatic occasions, he told us, "Jesus suffered too, but I did not suffer as much as Jesus because they took the needles out of my veins and the nails stayed in Jesus."

It became clear that Mark would die soon. We had several discussions with the family to prepare them for what now seemed inevitable. Some of the discussions included consideration of where he should die. Mark had been in the hospital so much over the past year that I felt he should die at home but I was concerned about his father. I felt that his mother, Ruth, would do well as she seemed to have deep spiritual convictions that were giving her strength. Eventually, we all agreed that Mark should be allowed to die at home surrounded by his family. We talked at length about what should be done and what should not be done if circumstances became too difficult for them.

Sometime before Mark's death, perhaps a month, he began to have recurrent dreams. One afternoon Brian asked if he could speak with me alone. He was extremely uneasy. Several days before, Mark had a dream in which he saw God. God had asked Mark if he wanted to be with him. The first time Mark told his father about the dream, Brian did not ask what Mark's answer was, but the last time he did. Mark said that his answer to God was "yes"—he wanted to be with God.

Days later Brian would again ask to speak with me about Mark's dreams but this time it was to relate that Mark had a dream in which he had been told by God the day he would die. Although I have strong spiritual beliefs, my scientific mind was highly skeptical. I stated that medically we did not know when Mark would die. It could be weeks or even months. The night before his dream-predicted death, Mark's parents called me several times even though there were no significant changes in his medical health.

Dr. Conte, a physician friend of mine, had gotten to know Mark and his family and, although he did not provide direct care for them, they had told him about Mark's dreams and the date that Mark said he would die. I arrived at the hospital hours after an early morning call from Brian. Dr. Conte met me shortly after I arrived and announced, "Well today is the day and Mark is still alive," in a tone as if to prove that Mark's dreams were not a real communication from God. "Phil," I said quietly, "Mark died two hours ago." Dr. Conte was stunned.

Months later as I reflected on Mark's life and death, I realized that Mark's father had called frequently the night before not because he wanted medical help, but because he was afraid that Mark's dream would come true. This would ultimately leave him with a dual challenge—the loss of his child and his own belief in God.

After the funeral service, the nurses and I were invited to Mark's home to see his room. Our contact with Mark had only been in the context of the hospital and so it seemed good to see where he lived when he was well. His room was warm and cheerful and filled with toys, all neatly arranged along with his hospital toys. There was a large poster of Batman to one side of his bed. We all sat on his bed, picked up the toys one by one, and talked about Mark. It was the first time we had openly shared our individual experiences about him. It was amazing to hear how many lives this four-year-old boy had touched in such a deep and meaningful way throughout his suffering.

We continued to sit there on his bed, talking about the picnic several weeks before Mark's death. While in the hospital, he asked if we could all have a picnic on the hospital grounds. Mark was in charge of this celebration. We honored his request. We sat in the middle of a small grass plot on a hospital blanket, myself and his nurses, with hospital personnel passing by and Mark tethered to an IV pole. Food and drinks included Teriyaki chicken, sourdough bread, and blackberry Mogen David wine. As our memories unfolded, our understanding increased, and we came to realize that Mark had prepared us for his "last supper" and his own death—communion in the true sense of the word.

As we were leaving Mark's home, his father told us that we were to take Mark's bicycle and other toys to the hospital. The day before his death Mark told Brian that the children in the hospital needed a good bike and he assigned toys to children he knew from the hospital. Even the day before his death he was concerned about others.

When Mark was alive and suffering, one of the questions his parents frequently asked me, and the one that was the most difficult to answer, was, "Why was Mark allowed to be born, if his life was only to become one of suffering and pain?" But Mark's life had instructed others and me. I was convinced that we should not question length of life, as if that is our only measure of a person's value. In the short years that Mark lived, he transmitted more love and understanding than many adults do over a lifetime. At the time of Mark's death his parents could not comprehend the profound meaning of his abbreviated life, but they, along with others, were to learn that Mark had imparted an enduring influence on people.

As I listen to the bittersweet story of Mark, I am stunned and speechless. I ask Arthur what impact Mark made on the rest of the medical community who cared for this little child.

THE LASTING IMPACT OF A LOST LIFE

Mark's influence actually persisted over the years. Many of us at the hospital spoke about Mark, remembering his smile, which had become a symbol of courage. His courage was to be a reminder to me over many years and through many painful times. If Mark, through his suffering, gave strength to others, then how could I get caught up in my own problems to the exclusion of others?

Thirty years have passed since Mark's death. His influence lives on today. Even now when I see a suffering or dying patient or have a friend who is critically ill and want to pass by the room or avoid talking about death, I hear the haunting statement that Mark once made, "Dr. Ammann doesn't come in to see me as much because he knows I am going to die." Whether in the hospital, in my community, with severely ill friends, or during my travels to developing countries, the words of Mark move me to embrace those who suffer the most. When I walk into a darkened African hut and encounter someone who is in pain and suffering—a mother, father, or child dying from AIDS—I hear Mark's voice and I reach out to touch them and feel the transforming spirit enter into both of us. Mark taught me that those who suffer are those who most need an embrace.

Over the years, I have spoken on many occasions about death and dying. Although I often quote from such great thinkers as Kubler-Ross, I never fail to talk about Mark and what he taught me about dying. Mark remained very visible to me throughout my life and his value to me never diminished. I don't know if it is possible to adequately answer the question, "How could God let a young infant be born only to suffer and die after a few years?," but I can say that Mark taught us that there is immense value in a life no matter how brief. When we discover that value, it can be used to help others and ourselves to confront the very meaning of life and death.

Many years after Mark's death, unanswered questions still linger about the mysteries of God's plans, especially with the death of a young child or a life abbreviated by a sudden tragic and seemingly unnecessary ending. There is one question that keeps coming to me—one that has become even more difficult than, "Why do some die young?" Is it possible that God could use (but not cause) the premature death of a child, or any person, as his message to those who are still living, so that we will have the strength to address the suffering of others? Does God in some way take the suffering of some—those things that seem to be so unjust to us—and transform it into strength for others? Does God, through the death of one, teach us the value of persons who are still living?

> [W]hen one man dies, one chapter is not torn out of the book, but translated into a better language; and every chapter must be so translated.[4]

No matter how one interprets Mark's life and death, or the life and death of any other child, I do know that he was an example of why Jesus told his disciples not to send the children away. We risk much when we deem

4. John Donne, Meditation XVII, in John Booty, ed., *John Donne: Selections from Divine Poems, Sermons, Devotions, and Prayers* (New York: Paulist, 1990), 271–72.

a child to be invisible. Jesus valued them. He not only wanted children to hear what he had to say, but he wanted his disciples to hear what the children had to say. If we are open, we can learn from even the youngest child. We can learn from a mind that is uncluttered by the complications of this world and, in the simplicity of a child's interpretation, see a glimpse of how God must see us and how we ought to see others. Mark was God's gift to me. Many learned from him just as other mothers and fathers must learn from their children.

> Jesus said," Let the little children come to me, and do not hinder them, for the kingdom heaven belongs to such as these." (Matt 19:14)

Practically any heartbreaking lesson we learn as parents is magnified as grandparents. The two of us begin relaying stories of our respective grandchildren and I soon realize that Arthur feels that he is just as likely to learn from them as he is to teach. This is illustrated by a story of his only granddaughter, Sophia.

My children and grandchildren taught me how to listen—to look into their eyes, to put down what I am reading, to turn off the noise of the world and focus on their singular needs—to enter their world of imagination, hear stories of fantasy, and take seriously their concerns and dreams. My own children were encouraging to me in times of weakness when I felt I should have shown them strength. They showed compassion and understanding during difficult times. They remain treasures, given to me by God not for me to keep forever but to return to their true Father, better for having been with me. How much more I could have learned from them had I listened more closely!

SOPHIA

I have often found that the best solutions come from the heart. Such was the case with Hope Walks, a program that was initiated by our foundation to help orphans and vulnerable children in poor countries.

The idea began in the heart of my granddaughter, Sophia. Just six years old at the time, Sophia had been watching her mother train for a breast cancer walk. When she asked if she could do the walk too, her mom told that she was too young. Frustrated, Sophia said, "But I want to do something to help the orphan children in Africa."

With her simple, emphatic statement Sophia planted the seed for Hope Walks. As a child she recognized what I had hoped adults would see: that there is a vast number of orphans throughout the world whose existence is nearly invisible and who need someone to discover their value and care enough to respond to their needs.

Because she was my granddaughter, Sophia was more aware of the orphan crisis than many adults are today. She knew I was a pediatrician who treated children infected by HIV. She realized I often traveled to Africa to help children and parents who had few resources to treat HIV or stop it from prematurely taking away their most precious possessions and their lives. She had seen videos about children who had lost their parents to AIDS or to rebel attacks on their villages. Hearing their stories and seeing their sadness had a deep effect on her still tender heart. She didn't want to just listen or watch, she wanted to do something to make the pain go away—and she didn't want to hear that she was too young.

These words from the Gospel express it well: "You have hidden these things from the wise and learned, and revealed them to little children" (Matt 11:25). After 25 years of the HIV epidemic, numbers like 15 million orphaned children or 6,100 more orphans each day are too hard for people to grasp. This reality needs to be brought home to adults by children in ways other than reciting numbers.

Sophia looked past the numbers into a deeper truth, a truth we adults shy away from. Instead of numbers, she saw children. Moreover, she saw them as children just like herself, and she knew how sad and scared she would be if she had HIV or if her mom or dad or both were dead, relegating her to an invisible life.

Sophia taught me that a child's will, driven by a loving heart, has all the strength needed to bring about change—if only we would listen. If one child has that much insight and compassion, imagine what could happen if thousands of other children had a chance to be heard like Sophia.

And so Hope Walks was born—a walk for children of all ages, from preschool through college. Its aim was to educate children and adults in countries with abundant resources about Africa's rapidly growing orphan crisis. Armed with that understanding and a sturdy pair of walking shoes, children and adults raised funds to support countless orphan programs to bring healthcare, food, shelter, and education to care for a child's body and mind. Equally important, they brought the realization that there are children in other parts of the world who are valuable enough for us to do something about their needs and to extend hope to those who seem hopeless—to bring them from invisible to visible.

It is amazing to me how much children of any age can accomplish. Today they also have a head start in their understanding and use of technology for tasks of grand scale. However, it is true that for every amazing, wonderful tool, there can be negative as well as positive outcomes. The effect of technology is a sensitive issue in our family, with the potential to harm as well as foster human relationships. I query Arthur about his thoughts and experiences with this issue and how he views the role of this in the valuation or devaluation of individuals. He responds with a desperate illustration.

TECHNOLOGY AND THE VALUE OF CHILDREN

Several months ago I watched a documentary about the impact of the Internet on parents and their children. I watched with great concern as I observed a modern-day version of the parable of the wayward son. I saw the painful effect that a teenager had on her parents as technology diverted her from a nurturing relationship with them to a dangerous interaction with an anonymous Internet predator, alienating her from her parents. There were promises of a virtual relationship that were destined to be devoid of love and compassion. Only when her extreme isolation mutated into despair, just short of suicide, did the child return into the arms and enduring love of her parents.

The documentary was a cautionary tale for parents and children alike. The Internet is capable of removing all traces of self-identity and can even become a tool of hatred and destruction. It is the responsibility of parents to monitor the use of technology to encourage and preserve the wonderful potential for learning and enrichment through this tool, while protecting them from any truly evil use of it. Relationships such as those between parents and children, once considered sacred, can become hidden in the "cloud," making them appear mundane and unimportant to a vulnerable child.

Children are our treasures and must be guarded. Increasingly, our society views children as objects, commodities, and targets of market forces. The outside world studies our children—how they think, how they react, what they like and dislike, what they buy, what they listen to, what they read and what they see. They intrude into every aspect of their lives, with or without permission. Outsiders view children as commodities for personal gain and not as individuals of value who are to be nurtured.

These are not reasons for parents to withdraw. Rather, these are reasons to protect our children, include them in our discussions, listen to their opinions, and provide them with the spiritual guidance that will help them survive even the most aggressive assaults on their integrity and spirituality. We must reject those who wish to destroy the foundations that have been laid by loving and caring mothers, fathers, and grandparents (as well as member of their extended family) who believe our children are on loan to us to be returned to God, better for having sojourned with us—not a cultural or marketing possession to be disposed of when no longer of value to the user.

For those who see children as nothing more than objects for personal use, economic gain, or even to exploit their minds or persuade them to abandon their spiritual beliefs, there are stern biblical warnings.

> And whoever welcomes one such child in my name welcomes me. But if anyone causes one of these little ones—those who believe in me—to stumble, it would be better for them to have a large millstone hung around their neck and to be drowned in the depths of the sea. (Matt 18:5–6)

We are surrounded by children, treasures that are not products of the materialistic world but of creation. Initially hidden from view during pregnancy, they become physically visible with their very first breath of life—their visibility and value increase with time. In the words of Jesus, "Truly I tell you, unless you change and become like little children, you will never enter the kingdom of heaven. Therefore, whoever takes the lowly position of this child is the greatest in the kingdom of heaven" (Matt 18:3–4).

We sit back in silence for a moment. Although we have covered a myriad of issues, we have hardly scratched the surface on this subject of generations and family. Beyond that, through our discussion the impact of Paul's declaration to Philemon—that Onesimus had become as a son to him—was beginning to sink in. The reality that Onesimus, once invisible to his master, was received and accepted as a son by Paul immediately brought to my mind a movement called Safe Families for Children, a concept that puts into action many of the beliefs that we had been discussing.

SAFETY WITHIN FAMILIES

I tell Arthur about my experience with a growing movement that is stepping into the gap to help families in crisis. At a recent event I heard incredible firsthand stories of families providing refuge for children at risk. I listened in fascination and awe as I heard volunteer families speak of how they are able to provide compassionate care for children of families in dire need until they can be safely returned. It was there that I realized that I was witnessing a graphic contemporary illustration of precisely what we have been discussing—Paul providing a temporary refuge for a runaway slave, Onesimus, and returning him to Philemon as a person of value. Here in Safe Families were thousands of "Pauls" opening their homes to even larger numbers of obscure, invisible, hurting children. Often a family is sidelined by reason of a mother or father in jail, a debilitating physical or mental illness, or devastating addictions—to name a few reasons. The child is quickly placed in the safe environment of a caring family, rather than into the complicated and expensive foster care system, giving relief and hope to all. The "invisible child" is now loved and nurtured, perhaps for the first time ever, as the treasure of which Jesus spoke. This action is an enactment of the scripture that declares in Jesus' own words, "Truly I tell you, whatever you did for one of the least of these brothers and sisters of mine, you did it for me" (Matt 25:40). In my own church I see over fifty families participating in this movement, and hear their reports of receiving rich blessing in the process.

I heard stories of children who were recipients of Safe Families care and who were transformed—given a new chance at life, becoming both visible and valuable. To me it affirmed the importance of each of us providing refuge for others and in the process discovering their value. This is not just an intellectual exercise, but a truth to be embraced and lived out.

THINK ON THESE THINGS

1. How can technology be used as a positive influence in family interaction? How can the overuse of technology disrupt family relationships? What boundaries are valuable in the use of technology in families?

2. What is the necessity of "letting go" of an individual within a family relationship? Why is it often difficult?

3. Describe an example or personal experience of a generational role reversal. What impact did it have?

4

Value between Wives and Husbands

Husbands, love your wives, just as Christ loved the church and gave
himself up for her to make her holy, cleansing her by the washing with
water through the word, and to present her to himself as a radiant church,
without stain or wrinkle or any other blemish, but holy and blameless. In
this same way, husbands ought to love their wives as their own bodies. He
who loves his wife loves himself. After all, no one ever hated their own body,
but they feed and care for their body, just as Christ does the church—for
we are members of his body. "For this reason a man will leave his father
and mother and be united to his wife, and the two will become one flesh."
This is a profound mystery—but I am talking about Christ and the church.
However, each one of you also must love his wife as he loves himself, and the
wife must respect her husband. (Eph 5:25–33)

We take a closer look at Paul's letter to Philemon and I am arrested by
one obvious "leave-out"—the subject of marriage. It is a natural omis-
sion for bachelor Paul, but one he boldly deals with in his other writings. Far from being obscure to him, he takes the marriage bond into a
deep spiritual relationship, making it highly visible by emphasizing the

shared value of each person. He elevates the sanctity and importance of marriage by using the analogy of Christ and the church.

We delve into some salient principles that arise between the lines in Paul's letter. This leads us deep into scriptural teachings of another unmarried man, Jesus. He connected the dots between himself and the church in a marriage metaphor, as well as the relationships of men and women. We reach for the Bible to shed more light on the subject.

> "Haven't you read," he replied, "that at the beginning the Creator 'made them male and female,' and said, 'For this reason a man will leave his father and mother and be united to his wife, and the two will become one flesh'? So they are no longer two, but one flesh. Therefore what God has joined together, let no one separate." (Matt 19:4–6)

Paul's letter to Philemon does not address the issue of marriage. His letter is a brief and compassionate communication in which he formulates his views on friendship, master and slave, father and son. Paul's ideas flowed from his renewed understanding of the Old Testament and the teachings of Jesus following his dramatic conversion. These teachings were solidified through his interaction with people he met in his travels—fellow Christians, apostles, male and female coworkers, and those with whom he underwent persecution in and out of prison. Paul was never married but the principles that he lays out in the letter to Philemon are applicable to all relationships. Applied to marriage, they form the basis for an enduring relationship that accommodates individuality between two highly different people, while simultaneously creating a lifelong bond between them. Through marriage, husbands and wives form the deepest and most complex of all relationships. It begins with an attraction between two physically and emotionally dissimilar individuals, and the relationship develops into a deep love, maturing into a profound spiritual and physical bond and incorporating sexual intimacy, the closest of physical experiences. Fundamentally, the husband and wife relationship calls for strength, understanding, commitment, and the recognition of the deep value of one another. Each must remain visible to the other and not be subsumed into a relationship of dominance.

MARILYN AND ARTHUR'S MARRIAGE

Marilyn and I met at Wheaton College, dated while I was in medical school, fell in love and decided to get married in spite of economic uncertainties. I needed to finish medical school and Marilyn's salary as a teacher was meager. On our wedding day, we recited vows that we had written. We labored over the words, taking each one seriously as we both acknowledged that our commitment to one another was for a lifetime. Like so many young couples, we were excited about our future but naïve about what it might bring, not anticipating some of the pain and suffering that would come and would require mutual support and understanding.

Perhaps our naïveté was an asset. We made most of the major decisions with very little information, including moving to California to accept a position as a pediatric resident at the University of California Medical Center in San Francisco. Marilyn accepted a teaching position at a high school in Daly City, California. We never visited any of these locations in advance. We simply packed up what we could in our 1955 DeSoto and raced the moving van from New Jersey to San Francisco.

During the formative years of marriage I do not recall disagreeing on any major decision. We always talked about what was best for each other and for the family. Marilyn's mother, her brother and his family, my sister and my aging parents all moved within a short distance from us. We were the oldest children in the greater family, giving us a position of daunting responsibility that taxed our own relationship with each other.

Difficult years came upon us. Marilyn's father died suddenly and her mother developed Alzheimer's disease at an early age. It progressed relentlessly to the point where she needed constant attention. Marilyn was a faithful daughter, visiting her mother with increasing frequency as she deteriorated. My parents were aging and unable to take full responsibility for their own care or for my sister, who had lifelong schizophrenia, which disrupted family relationships. There were times when we felt that we could not take on one more responsibility without threatening our own relationship, and were it not for the value we found in each other and our deep spiritual commitment, our marriage could have suffered significantly.

As we moved past our fiftieth wedding anniversary, we reflected back on our marriage and saw it as one where our willingness to adapt to difficult circumstances provided the stability that we needed to remain close. Like Paul with Onesimus, we saw value in our relationship to one another and to each individual who came into our path. That was translated into the caring that we provided for those in need, even when it meant giving up some of our own needs. We believe that we are still discovering value in one another and in others—a process we hope will continue for many more years.

A myriad of books and manuals written on pre-marriage counseling and marriage itself attest to the difficulties encountered in husband-wife relationships. It is difficult in contemporary culture to discuss marriage without entering into some sort of controversy. Dominant today is a discussion regarding same-sex marriages, a discussion that is as much about political agendas as it is legalities. It is not surprising therefore that, to many, it is a discussion about the deterioration of the sanctity of marriage as presented throughout the Old and New Testament. Once the sacredness of the marriage commitment, originally a spiritual covenant, devolved into a secular and government-controlled contract, the trajectory could only be towards a legalistic view of marriage that focuses increasingly on material benefits such as property rights, inheritance, and ownership of children. A marriage relationship is more than mere friendship, although this may be one of the strengthening bonds of marriage. It is also greater than the genetic relationship of brother and sister or parent and child. It is certainly more than a contractual agreement between two interested parties, although this may be required by the church and state to recognize the legitimacy of the marriage. For those who believe in the spiritual foundation of marriage, the absence of a spiritual relationship between a husband and wife is telling. Under these circumstances the deterioration of marriage into a legalistic relationship is not surprising.

It seems sad to me that marriage has become primarily a contractual agreement after such a long history of being a covenant relationship.

The challenge arises of how to establish the commitment level of two individuals to recognize the value and purpose of one another.

COVENANT OR CONTRACT—HISTORICAL VIEWS

As with many changes in our society, those with influence generate theories that are often self-serving and distort the value of an individual. Christianity was not immune from such practices. In the early church Augustine and Aquinas both looked at the purpose of marriage as primarily intended for procreation. The emphasis on procreation came from a focus on Genesis 1 and a natural law interpretation of "be fruitful and multiply."

Martin Luther held to these views, maintaining that there were two kingdoms in which Christians were destined to live: the earthly or political kingdom, and the heavenly or spiritual kingdom. He believed marriage belonged to the earthly kingdom, contributing to subjugating marriage to legal and state controls.

Subsequent interpretations of marriage came from many sources, but especially from Puritan theology and an understanding that focused on Genesis 2—the creation of woman out of man. Their theology emphasized the interdependent relationship between husband and wife as reciprocal and not unilateral, e.g., not inferior versus superior or subservient versus dominant. Man and woman were created first, before procreation occurred. The Puritans saw mutuality in the Genesis creation story as help for one another. Children were the result or by product, not the purpose of the union.

As we dig deeper into the Genesis account of creation, it becomes obvious how far our culture has drifted from the original intentions. In addition, Arthur's interest in history brings some fascinating quotes to the surface.

> The LORD God said, "It is not good for the man to be alone. I will make a helper suitable for him."
>
> Now the LORD God had formed out of the ground all the wild animals and all the birds in the sky. He brought them to the man to see what he would name them; and whatever the man called each living creature, that was

45

its name. So the man gave names to all the livestock, the birds in the sky and all the wild animals.

But for Adam no suitable helper was found. So the LORD God caused the man to fall into a deep sleep; and while he was sleeping, he took one of the man's ribs and then closed up the place with flesh. Then the LORD God made a woman from the rib he had taken out of the man, and he brought her to the man.

The man said, "This is now bone of my bones and flesh of my flesh; she shall be called 'woman,' for she was taken out of man."

That is why a man leaves his father and mother and is united to his wife, and they become one flesh. (Gen 2:18–24)

Historically, several legalists and theologians pointed out that the social and community importance of marriage was in sharp contrast to contemporary views of marriage as an independent contract between two individuals whose relationship has little to do with others or the building of family and community. In the late 1800s, Chancellor James Kent, an organizer of American common law, wrote about the social importance and spirituality of the marriage relationship

The primary and most important of the domestic relations is that of husband and wife. It has its foundations in nature, and is the only lawful relation by which Providence has permitted the continuance of the human race. In every age it has had a propitious influence on the moral improvement and happiness of humankind. It is one of the chief foundations of social order. We may justly place to the credit of the institution of marriage a great share of the blessings which flowed from the refinement of manners, the education of children, the sense of justice, and cultivation of the liberal arts.[5]

---

5. James Kent, *Commentaries on American Law*, ed. Oliver Wendell Holmes Jr., 12th ed. (Boston: Little, Brown, 1896), 276.

Unraveling these various historic views of marriage, we decide it is time to go back and trace the foundations taught by Paul, which reveal many layers and dimensions that relate to marriage.

The Apostle Paul understood the marriage relationship in two very different dimensions. One in terms of creation—when a man and woman agree to marriage and they commit to explore their own spiritual depth. The other dimension, in terms of a "mystery," is where he likens the relationship of Christ and the church to that of a groom and bride. A married couple experiences a deeper dimension in their commitment to one another in the light of Christ's relationship to the church. This link to the church as Christ's bride widens their world and they seek not only the value of each other in physical and spiritual dimensions but also their joint value to the church.

> Husbands, love your wives, just as Christ loved the church and gave himself up for her to make her holy, cleansing her by the washing with water through the word, and to present her to himself as a radiant church, without stain or wrinkle or any other blemish, but holy and blameless. In this same way, husbands ought to love their wives as their own bodies. He who loves his wife loves himself. After all, no one ever hated their own body, but they feed and care for their body, just as Christ does the church— for we are members of his body. "For this reason a man will leave his father and mother and be united to his wife, and the two will become one flesh." This is a profound mystery—but I am talking about Christ and the church. However, each one of you also must love his wife as he loves himself, and the wife must respect her husband. (Eph 5:25–33)

Paul's view of marriage is grounded in the historical perspective of Old Testament teaching and what he observed as a leader in Jewish society and Christian churches, though not from personal experience. In his newfound relationship with Christ, he places marriage at the highest spiritual level with the understanding that the marriage relationship describes both the relationship between a husband and wife and the relationship of Christ with the church. Through Paul, we are given insight into the mystery of marriage. This marriage metaphor of Christ as the Bridegroom and the church as the bride is at the same time beautiful, mysterious, simple, and yet very complex. To embrace it fully is to bask in the truth that we, as believers, are loved!

Using the words "mysterious" and "complex" bring to my mind connotations of other teachings that have been misinterpreted and misused to the detriment of women through the centuries. Again our conversation delves deeper into current issues.

Without simultaneously considering the creation story along with the teachings of both Jesus and Paul, misleading conclusions may be drawn. A portion of Paul's teaching quoted below has caused the devaluation, pain, and suffering of women, especially married women, worldwide. "Wives, submit yourselves to your own husbands as you do to the Lord. For the husband is the head of the wife as Christ is the head of the church, his body, of which he is the Savior. Now as the church submits to Christ, so also wives should submit to their husbands in everything" (Eph 5:22–24). Many stop there and do not go on to observe the next paragraph where husbands are told to "love your wives, just as Christ loved the church and gave himself up for her. . . . In the same way, husbands ought to love their wives as their own bodies . . ." (Eph 5:25, 28).

Again, these words of Paul must be considered simultaneously with those of the Genesis story, where God created man and woman with equal authority over his creation and where his intent was that the two should become one.

> Then God said, "Let us make mankind in our image, in our likeness, so that they may rule over the fish in the sea and the birds in the sky, over the livestock and all the wild animals, and over all the creatures that move along the ground."
>
> So God created mankind in his own image, in the image of God he created them; male and female he created them. (Gen 1:26–27)

Later in Genesis we are told that the relationship between man and woman is mutual companionship, "The LORD God said, 'It is not good for the man to be alone. I will make a helper suitable for him'" (Gen 2:18). In his letter to the Ephesians, Paul did not deviate from his teaching of the value of others. However, like Jesus, he took the teachings of the Old Testament and increased the responsibility of individuals to each other. Paul makes this clear in this passage:

> "For this reason a man will leave his father and mother and be united to his wife, and the two will become one flesh." This is a profound mystery—but I am talking about Christ and the church. However, each one of you also must love his wife as he loves himself, and the wife must respect her husband. (Eph 5:31–33)

Again I realize that Arthur's extensive medical work with women worldwide has uniquely sensitized him to their plight of abuse and suffering. He has witnessed extremes and it comes through strongly as we discuss crucial issues. He graphically portrays much of this in his book *Women, HIV, and the Church: In Search of Refuge* (Cascade Books, 2012). Unfortunately, we need only to look as far as the morning news to find examples of abuse in marriage.

MISINTERPRETATIONS ABOUND

The relationship between husbands and wives is compared to Christ as head of the church, and Christ giving himself up for the church. Paul implies that this is an extraordinary responsibility between husbands and wives, but especially for the husband. The teaching of Paul in the letter to Philemon is an extension of the basic teaching of Jesus about the marriage relationship. Simply put, each person, whether slave or master, wife or husband, must view the other person as being highly visible and of such great value that they are willing to give up what they possess, including their own life, for that person.

The misinterpretation of the teachings of Jesus and Paul results in the perpetuation of counter-spiritual attitudes of inferiority and subjugation of women to men. This is a part of almost every culture and religion. It has been disastrous for women. Physical, emotional, sexual, and spiritual abuse abound as women are deprived of their basic rights and fundamental value. Yet, it is widely acknowledged that women are essential for the cohesiveness and survival of cultures, societies, and families. Degradation of women results in deterioration of social and spiritual values and ultimately of family and society.

If we believe in the value of a person, we need to champion the worth of each individual. This applies especially to women, who are too often degraded and abused. And lest we become smug, supposing that degrading attitudes toward women are not pervasive in our own culture, in and out of marriage, we only need to spend fifteen minutes watching late-night television, watch one R-rated movie, listen to the first few lines of a rap song, view the marketing of sexuality to young girls and boys, surf the Internet, or read about the success of the pornography industry. Even the smallest "Hometown USA" is subject to the degradation of women in abusive and shocking terms. No place is exempt. Jesus recognized the inherent value of women and therefore did not exclude them in any manner from his ministries; in fact he often placed women at the forefront as he walked and taught.

The genealogy of Jesus includes women. In her recent book *The Greatest Gift: Unwrapping the Full Love Story of Christmas*, Ann Voskamp traces the lineage of Christ. In his day only men were listed in genealogies, never women. She writes:

> It was in that time of prophets and kings, the time of Mary and Joseph, that men were in genealogies and women were invisible. But for Jesus, women had names and stories and lives that mattered.
>
> The family tree of Christ startlingly notes not one woman but four. Four broken women—women who felt like outsiders, like has-beens. Women who were weary of being taken advantage of, of being unnoticed and uncherished and unappreciated: women who didn't fit in, who didn't know how to keep going, what to believe, where to go—women who had thought about giving up. And Jesus claims exactly these who are wandering and wondering and wounded and worn out as His.[6]

6. Ann Voskamp, *The Greatest Gift: Unwrapping the Full Love Story of Christmas* (Carol Stream, IL: Tyndale, 2013), ix.

Through Jesus' eyes, women were made visible!

The importance of the mutuality of women and men is magnified by Jesus' acceptance of women, an exception in his culture, where women were considered to be of low status. His example informs us that for a marriage to endure today both husband and wife must be intentional and unconditional in their commitment to one another, creating a spiritual depth like that of Christ in his relationship with his beloved church. Their commitment must extend to even the most difficult circumstances, as is often identified in wedding vows. Not merely a theoretical notion, the promise that is spoken "in sickness and in health . . . as long as we both shall live" includes possible life-threatening illness, which brings a jolting reality to their very mortality.

From his comment about serious illness, I sense that Arthur is speaking from experience. Although I know very few details of Arthur and Marilyn's lives since our early years of college, I asked if there was a particular experience he is referring to.

A WALK NOT OF OUR OWN CHOOSING

My wife and I like to walk. We don't do it often enough. But there was a walk that we embarked on that neither of us had planned or would have chosen.

As a physician, countless times I sat wearing a white coat as a symbol of medical authority, peering into anxious faces. The eyes stared back at me pleading for good news but I had none to give.

Tumor, growth, mass. These were substitute words to soften the truth. Reality did not set in until the real words were slowly mouthed: cancer, malignancy. When it did, confusion and fear were simultaneously triggered.

Now it was my turn to be seated opposite the man in the white coat, alongside Marilyn, my beloved. The constant mixture of good and bad news unraveled.

Yes, malignant, but it could be slow-growing.

Yes, metastatic, but only one lymph node involved.

Yes, there are side effects of treatment, but treatment is so much better now.

Yes, the five-year survival rate is good, but recurrences are very difficult to treat.

Weeks into the diagnosis of metastatic breast cancer, with seemingly endless physician visits and information, like the Internet, overwhelmed my brain with too much information—it still did not seem real. Like a movie that is seen over and over and over again, each time there was something new, and yet it was all there at the beginning. Somehow, immersed in the midst of all the details, the most important factor had been obscured.

My love and I would go for a walk, a journey that neither of us had chosen.

Suffering is painful, but it is like a wound drawing out healing from within. Marilyn's closest friends offered themselves and their understanding. Conversations, physical presence, prayers—the very spiritual strength that we draw on when those we love feel our pain. Our children, Kim and Scott, always so precious to us and so often our concern, were now adults whose faces and questions betrayed their concern beyond words that they expressed. Sophia, our grandchild, was there to bring joy to the one who was suffering.

We sat on the couch as the morning sun broke through the partially open blinds. All the medical studies were completed. All the opinions were given. The decision for chemotherapy and radiation had been made.

Fear began to set in. It was easy to express it on this quiet morning. Treatment might result in fatigue, depression, loss of hair, changed schedules, and cancellation of events.

Would people understand? Would it all be in vain and death be inevitable? Would our love remain strong? Would our love endure? (How could such a thought occur?) And yet I understood the questions and doubts as I realized that fear comes as we face our own immortality and that of others near and dear to us.

There was softness on that morning as we held hands and looked at one another. I had often wondered why I had lived so many years. Why so many times had I come so close to death and yet survived. I could utter the words that I felt. "I am alive today because God has allowed me to be here to care for you."

In my heart I prayed, "Dear God take away her fear and let me be a part of her strength to overcome whatever we will encounter. You know the future and whether our lives together will be long or short, peaceful or sorrowful."

I am stunned and teary-eyed in silence as this story unfolds. It has been twelve years since Arthur prayed that prayer. He now speaks softly as he imparts insight from this painful path they walked together.

This was not the only struggle that we had in over fifty years of marriage. There were other events that tested our relationship, sometimes to the depth of wondering how we could absorb more stress, which increases with aging. But we were always committed to one another and that seemed to be the difference. Rabbi Ohriner summarized it well at a wedding I recently attended. "In contracts we share duties. In covenants we shared destiny." Certainly, marriage should not be like a contract that can be easily broken when something goes wrong. Just as God was committed to a covenant to his people, so too in marriage we are committed to a relationship that endures.

Many relationships between husbands and wives require unequal sacrifice that can only be made if each person sees value in the other. Too often, driven by culture, tradition, or religion, the woman is called on to make the greater or the more frequent sacrifice. The teachings of Jesus and Paul state that it is a husband's responsibility, in love and mutuality, to recognize the value of his wife. As years pass in a marriage the question of both husband and wife should be, "Have I recognized the value of my spouse and allowed her/him to be a better person for having been with me, or have we somehow drifted into being invisible to one another?"

A lasting marriage is not easily achieved. No voluntary relationship other than marriage is called upon to endure the vicissitudes of vast life changes. Two people initially attracted to one another without really knowing the complexity of their personalities, journey through life to meet challenges that may exceed those of any other relationship. To endure, there must be accommodation and adjustment to change. Marriages have many stories and plots within each story. Initially there are two young people little more than strangers, trying to understand and adjust to what each one may have brought to their union. Their relationship continues through magnitudes of change that include finances, education, spiritual values, political issues, professions, social contacts, relocation, job changes, new friends or loss of old friends, and perhaps the greatest of all challenges, the raising of children. Add to that list changes that occur with aging, physical, political, social, philosophical, spiritual, birth and death events. Truly deep relationships, designed by God, require a willingness to give up something. The human tendency is to want to keep it all or to keep part of it as if a relationship such as marriage is a game of who wins out. The counterintuitive teachings of Jesus portray the opposite—giving up what a person has for the sake of others—and by giving up something, a person gains. Under ideal circumstances this is understood by both husband and wife. Under distorted circumstances this is interpreted as one person, usually the husband, requiring that the wife be submissive. The teachings of Jesus do not permit such an interpretation. Jesus, in fact, turned the historical worldview of women upside down when he associated with women, spoke to them as individuals, and defended even the prostitute and the adulterous woman against the male dominance of his time.

The theology of the marriage relationship between a husband and wife was established in the creation story. Neither Jesus nor Paul deviated from the concept of an enduring covenant of shared responsibility, mutual respect and recognizing the value of an individual. Jesus increased the responsibility between marriage partners, emphasizing its permanence. Paul in his writing to the Ephesians amplified the spiritual significance of the bond between a husband and wife by using the analogy of the relationship between Christ and the church.

We reflect on responses we each have received when we tell someone that our individual marriages have lasted for over fifty years. Often, especially with younger people, there is an expression of amazement stating, "We don't know of anyone that has been married that long!" It is an opportunity to express our shared belief that marriage is more than a contract—it is a covenant embracing a shared spiritual destiny where each person becomes more and more visible. As our understanding and sharing with one another expands and increases, we are free to remove any "masks" we hide behind. We then become more authentic and transparent and, yes, more visible and valuable to one another.

THINK ON THESE THINGS

1. What is the importance of understanding marriage as a covenant versus a contract?

2. How does Paul's connection of marriage with the image of Christ and the church enlarge your thinking of the marriage relationship? What insight have you gained in thinking about yourself as the bride of Jesus?

3. What do you think are the greatest challenges to the marriage relationship today?

4. What advice would you give to a young couple on how best to have a marriage that recognizes the value of each other? How can older couples continue to value each other?

5

Barriers to Discovering True Value

*I am sending him—who is my very heart—back to you. I would have
liked to keep him with me so that he could take your place in helping me
while I am in chains for the gospel. But I did not want to do anything
without your consent, so that any favor you do would not seem forced but
would be voluntary. Perhaps the reason he was separated from you for
a little while was that you might have him back forever—no longer as a
slave, but better than a slave, as a dear brother. He is very dear to me but
even dearer to you, both as a fellow man and as a brother in the Lord.*
(Phlm 12–16)

This chapter is not about developing a new system of power and control
that is more just, or a new system of national or global economics that is
more equitable. Nor is it about favoring one political system over another
or one economic system over another. It is about what happens to individuals within a relationship or system when the value of the individual is
demeaned or lost. When that happens, it initiates the pathway to failure of
families, communities, religious organizations, governments, and even the
whole of society.

We talk for a long time about the master-slave relationship of Philemon and Onesimus. How did circumstances between them become so desperate that this slave was driven to risk his very life by first stealing something from his master and then running away some 1,200 miles from Colossae to Rome? The gulf between them was more than a matter of master and slave, as we first supposed, but involved the much broader ethical issues of justice and equity, wealth and poverty, power and control (promoting superiority), prominence and insignificance, fame and obscurity, visibility and invisibility.

In virtually every culture and society, issues of superiority and inferiority exist. If they don't exist, given time, someone will surely invent some identifier that can be used to distinguish between a presumed superior and a supposedly inferior being. Whether it is belonging to the right tribe, speaking the right language, having extreme wealth, holding political power, being of a certain skin color, possessing an academic degree from a prestigious university, having a heritage of royalty, being born into a privileged class, or being male or female, humankind is adept at developing a means to claim domination over another individual. Often in relationships where there are superiors in authority and thus inferiors below, there is also a question of justice and equity which complicates the equation as well.

The teachings of Jesus break through these artificial distinctions, and Paul's letter to Philemon carries out his teaching. His relationship with Onesimus illustrates the extraordinary results of considering innate value of a person of low estate.

Something went very wrong with the relationship between Philemon and Onesimus, who fled the household in which he lived and worked. Philemon was the master and Onesimus was his servant, but more than that—he was a slave.

Philemon was an influential and powerful religious leader who was fully aware of social and spiritual needs of the people who surrounded him. Paul tells us that Philemon was known for his love and faith to fellow Christians and for his ministry of helping others. He gained the respect of Paul and the community as a spiritual leader. Yet it seems that Philemon was unaware of Onesimus and his needs. Although it appears that

Onesimus was considered invisible to Philemon, the very name Onesimus is derived from the Greek word meaning beneficial or profitable. How could these two individuals Philemon and Onesimus have missed one another so completely while they were in the same household, especially during a time when Philemon was actively engaged in a Christian ministry and building the church?

What went wrong in their relationship is perhaps a mirror of what happens in the impersonal atmosphere of our current culture, where a great divide exists in relationships between those in authority those who are subordinates. No matter what the relationship may be—brothers, sisters, husbands and wives, friends or children, this issue of domination hides in the background ready to emerge and disrupt, demean or depreciate. It may happen insidiously or suddenly, but all too often the end result deems a person to be invisible.

I see that Arthur has particularly strong feelings about this and I am curious to know if a life experience has precipitated his emotion. Indeed it has!

AN IMPORTANT EARLY LESSON

I well remember an unpleasant experience that I had as a sixteen-year-old when I was employed in a Christian camp for a summer job—an experience that forcefully imprinted on me how power (authority, dominance) can obscure the value of an individual.

My Christianity was scarcely more than two years old when, as a high school student, I went to work at a summer Christian camp in the Adirondack Mountains of New York. As a young follower of Christ, I was eager to participate in new experiences and I trusted that among Christians the experiences would all be positive. Many of the counselors that I met during the summer were sensitive to the needs of others. They were models whose example I tried to follow. But unknown to me, the founder of the camp, a prominent and well-known evangelist, had a personal agenda and readily used young people to foster his personal goal of becoming an even more highly recognized Christian leader. I arrived at the camp full of enthusiasm and trust. The setting was idyllic. It was located on an island in the middle of a lake high in the Adirondacks and accessible only by boat. From the shore it looked like an emerald green thickly wooded forest . When I arrived on the island after a short boat ride I immediately felt the spirit of the camp. Largely as the result of enthusiastic workers and counselors, physical activities for the campers, and evening worship and singing of hymns, within days my sense of inspiration accelerated. However, I soon observed that numbers were important to the founder of the camp—the number attending the camp each week, the number of converts, and, to accommodate the ever increasing number of campers, the number of new cabins that had to be built. To achieve his goals he had to exploit young inexperienced Christians on his staff.

It affected me personally. The problem was that there were only two carpenters and my primary job at age sixteen was to help build new cabins. We were expected to complete one cabin each week to accommodate the ever-increasing number of new campers. No camp worker had a single job, including me. Building cabins was my daytime occupation. In the evening everyone, including myself, also functioned as a counselor. This included an evening Bible study for which preparation was necessary. Then there was the cleanup assignment. Mine included washing the sinks and toilets in the common area. Finally, there were daily staff meetings and mandatory attendance at the evening worship services.

Toward the end of the summer, fatigue set in and I got sick—terribly sick. I don't remember much about the illness, only that it began with severe chills and merged into a semi-comatose state after which the camp nurse finally had to take me home. It was a six-hour drive to New York City. I was unaware of the trip and never woke up until three days later. During my time at the camp, during the illness, and following recovery I never was visited or called by the camp founder. I felt as invisible to him as Onesimus was to Philemon. After I recovered I later learned that I was more fortunate than my friend George. He was also a teenager and his roles were as a mechanic and a motor boatman. One of his duties was to ferry campers and their luggage from the mainland to the island. George also kept the generators running during the day as they were only source of electricity for the entire island. Over the summer I had gotten to know George well. He was quiet in disposition, tall with striking blonde hair, and had a muscular build that suited him well to his assigned tasks. I never heard him complain. Because of George's large muscular appearance he was often asked, even though a teenager, to do more than he was physically capable of doing.

The last week of camp, after all the campers had left, George had the responsibility of closing up camp for the winter. All of the remaining supplies were loaded into a converted, used military vessel propelled by an outboard motor. This was the one last trip to the mainland for the season.

There were several problems with George's last trip. The boat was overloaded and it was not approved or licensed for heavy loads, and George was given no life jacket although it was known that he could not swim—details that seemed to concern no one. On his last trip across the lake the water was exceptionally choppy. With the extremely heavy load, the front of the vessel suddenly plunged underwater. There was no one onboard to save George. He was alone and far from shore. He drowned!

We sit in stunned silence as the reality of this event settles over us. I question Arthur as to what impact this had upon him as a formative teen.

That experience ran through my brain over and over again for many years. To this day I remember the details vividly. Here was a camp that was established to meet the needs of young people just like George and me. Every week they came, all summer long from all over New York State. But individuals like George who served and who made it all possible were unrecognized and unacknowledged. George was unknown to the camp founder, who was, however, proudly recognized for his ministry to young people. Unfortunately, he used the naïveté of young Christians for personal gain, violated age and work rules for employment, disregarded human health and safety standards, and betrayed a spiritual trust to value all those in his path. George was like a modern-day Onesimus. His value never registered with the camp founder, who was too busy talking about Christian values.

This happens in today's big business culture as well. Losing sight of the value of an individual is relatively easy under circumstances where a hierarchy of authority or power exists. In fact, it is often justified as a means of protecting the time of the person in authority so that all their efforts can be devoted to a singular goal or task. If problems exist with an individual employee, it may be deferred to a human resource department or to an individual in an intermediate position. Today, the higher up the boss, the more often he or she is unaware, perhaps deliberately, of the daily struggles of those beneath. Working conditions, salaries, vacations, retirement benefits, safety, education, and healthcare are known perhaps only in the context of an impersonal quarterly or annual corporate report. A request for an increase in salary may be judged solely in terms of efficiency or productivity, devoid of consideration for need or work conditions. The corporate spreadsheet is not programmed to compute the personal needs of an employee even if desperate and life-threatening circumstances exist or even if the entire health and well-being of a family is at stake. The rationalization at the top may be that there are always government and social programs to deal with these kinds of problems or that learning about an individual's personal needs has nothing to do with conducting business. The mantra of the person in power is often, "My only responsibility is the profitability of the company so that the investors are happy." The system is established on principles devoid of justice and equity.

We talk further about several instances, even in Arthur's medical career, in what might be called "big business" or "corporate life," when he experienced this sort of behavior.

I first became aware of how insidiously depersonalization of others can occur during my own career at the university and subsequently while working at a prominent biotechnology company. In both situations I managed physicians, technicians, secretaries, nurses, and research fellows—perhaps twenty or more individuals at any one time. It seemed easier to isolate myself from troubling issues by dealing with everyone equally according to the rules and protecting myself from extraneous issues, which I defined as "personal problems." I rationalized that this would allow me to do my job better as a physician and researcher. I must admit it was more efficient to hide behind the rules of a bureaucracy of black-and-white rules than to address the personal struggles or problems of an employee. Not knowing about their personal lives meant there was no need to act, an approach that anesthetized my emotions and took away any potential of pain that might get messy or result from becoming deeply involved in anything beyond the business of the day. I was behaving precisely like Philemon, who had ignored the value of Onesimus, not realizing that the people traveling in my sphere of influence had been placed there for another purpose as well. It was mine to discover their intrinsic value and look beyond just their job performance. I could not simply choose to use them and ignore who they were. And I soon learned that who they were as people was as much or more important than their age or professional skills. They were my helpers, individuals who came with their skills to help me succeed. But they also came with problems, concerns, struggles and pains, and spouses and children, which I couldn't ignore. Individuals in authority often make conscious decisions about who is valuable enough to spend time with or to invest in and who might somehow remain invisible. Philemon's failure to recognize Onesimus may have been that he never considered that there was any value in pursuing a deeper relationship with someone in such a lowly position. What could a slave offer him as a Christian leader? Certainly not prestige or money or increased power. But Paul saw something different. He saw Onesimus as a person of value.

This precipitates more questions about how this applies today. What about leadership training to sharpen awareness and importance of people on every "rung of the ladder"? How might those in authority learn to recognize and preserve value in each individual? What could promote an invisible person to be discovered and seen as valuable?

Take corporations for example. Many executives manage a corporation without taking the time to develop their leadership skills—taking courses, listening to lectures, or reading books about management and interpersonal relationships. If they do, or if a corporation requires it, the material frequently consists of how to avoid sexual harassment, how to fire an employee, how to protect the company from liability, and how to rationalize why the company's welfare is more important than the employee. The needs of the employee and their family are discounted. Managers are discouraged from becoming involved in personal matters. It would be an amazing transformation if businesspersons or professionals in any field were to view their employees as Jesus did. It is unlikely that there would be any Enron, WorldCom, or government gridlock debacles. I doubt that there would be forty-one million people without health insurance in the United States. There would not be individuals suffering alone and in silence because their work overwhelms them and their families, or their salaries are insufficient to provide for the essentials of living. Individuals would not be losing their homes because they were viewed merely as commodities in a chain of impersonal economic events. You cannot value a person and at the same time take financial advantage of him or her especially when great disparities in status exist. A little research demonstrates that this is not a new problem, but one that is scattered throughout the history of humanity.

ARE THEY BETTER OFF?

> Now, according to St. Thomas Aquinas, the economic order should be organized in a diametrically different fashion: the needs of man *must* determine economic priorities. What man needs is neither an ever-increasing cash flow nor a continually expanding investment portfolio, but rather a society that gives him a chance to procure what he needs for himself and his family, and to use what he procures virtuously. He needs a society that looks after the Common Good, which, by definition, would be a society that places his fundamental needs and those of his fellow-citizens—and *not* those of merchants, bankers, and bureaucrats—at the center of economic organization. From the spiritual point of view, those economic needs must be satisfied in such a way as to secure that most important of all retirement plans: Eternity.[7]

One of the principles contained in Paul's letter to Philemon, and one that we also read about in the teachings of Jesus, is that we are to acknowledge the basic needs of those who fall within our sphere of influence—whether a parent, an employer, an employee, a friend, or a stranger. This principle should revolutionize the thinking of all Christians who find themselves in a position of superior authority, wealth, or power. Somehow the rich, famous, and powerful must learn that those whom society may view as subservient or marginal are to be viewed as human beings of equal value. Those who find themselves in positions of authority, control, or wealth have acquired it

7. The Directors, "Preface," in G. K. Chesterton, *The Outline of Sanity* (Norfolk, VA: IHS Press, 2001), 15.

not only for their own benefit but for the benefit of others. Each of us must ask ourselves certain critical questions. Is the worker better off for having worked for me? Is my employer better off for my having worked for them? These are questions that need to be extended to all relationships: Is my child better for having been parented by me even though I am in a position of control? Are my parents better for having raised me? Are my students of greater value because of what I have taught them?

I sense that an emerging factor is one's willingness to become personally involved with others. There is no substitute for genuine concern and understanding, not to be confused with a quantified philosophy of redistribution of wealth, of socialism or of capitalism. Arthur takes it a step further.

It takes effort and time to go beyond the routine greeting of "How are you?" And when the reply is "Not so good," it may require taking the risk of going deeper and trying to find the issue in that person's life. Going deeper means getting involved. People at the "top" by any definition often don't like to get involved with those whom they may deem invisible. So often, after the painful separation of a husband and wife or parent and child, or an employee who resigns in ill health, we hear, "I never knew anything was wrong" or "It came as a complete surprise." We even hear it after a suicide when a close relative or friend says, "I never knew there was a problem." Is it possible that two people can live together and yet be so far apart? Is it possible for two people to interact and never be aware that there are deep internal struggles? Is the pattern in our culture to isolate and insulate the influential and wealthy from the invisible sector of the weak and the poor?

A DIFFERENT MODEL—THE WAY OF JESUS

Jesus is not a typical role model for the corporate executive who is driven to maximize exposure to the most important people, or the politician fighting to meet the greatest number of people to get the most votes. Jesus met people— often individuals—day or night, in crowds or alone. He was living water to meet the spiritual and physical needs of a solitary outcast woman. His words could be understood by those who knew their need of God but confounded those who were merely curious. He unveiled profound truths to the poor and needy but often hid spiritual secrets from the powerful religious leaders of his day. In reality, Jesus had far more significance than the world's richest investors, the world's most powerful political leaders, and the world's most successful corporate executives. Yet, he focused not on the successful and influential, but on the poor and needy even at the expense of his own life. Looking back at history it is clear that the one who is most remembered and the one who remains the most influential is the one who was truly humble about his own position. It is human nature to stratify individuals. Like associates with like. Individuals of the academy look down and devalue those who are uneducated as not having the intellectual capacity to understand complex issues. Wealthy individuals socialize and live in certain neighborhoods, sometimes with clear-cut boundaries, where they attend the same clubs, travel in the same circles, and indulge in similar activities. Often their view is expressed as, "I made it; they can too." Politically powerful people keep their distance from ordinary people even though their mandate is to serve the public. "Public servant" has been expunged from the vocabulary of many politicians for the sake of power. When individuals put distance between themselves and those who they judge to be of lesser value, they miss some of most rewarding experiences that can only occur when we interact with someone who is indeed quite different than ourselves.

We pause in the conversation. This seems to be the most complex subject we have discussed so far, and I want to get my arms around it in practical language. I question whether this is a one-way street or if there is benefit to be gained on both sides of the power curve.

A VERY SPECIAL CAB RIDE

I make it a habit to talk to cab drivers. Often they are from foreign countries and always they have opinions about their own countries and their view of the US. For many, it is the only job they can get while they try to support their family or go to school to advance their education. For me, it is always an opportunity to learn. Early one morning I had to go to downtown Manhattan. The cab and driver you get is of course pure chance. This time the driver was black and spoke with a distinct accent which I recognized. "Are you from Haiti?" I inquired. Surprised, he asked if I had ever been to Haiti. I replied that all I knew about Haiti came from two sources: the pastor of music at my church, who went there every year to learn about and teach music and who relayed to us the wonderful sounds of Haitian music, and the wonderful people whom I met on our visits to the Haitian Bateyes in the Dominican Republic. As we navigated the crowed and noisy streets of Manhattan, the conversation that followed was all about Haiti, its people, its culture and music. After we reached our destination I sat in the cab and continued the conversion. As I left the cab he said to me, "Sir, thank you for telling me all the good things about Haitians. You see, here in New York we are not always viewed positively. This morning before I left my home to start work I prayed that one of my passengers would be a person who saw the good in us. My prayer has been answered." What a blessing his words were to me, that I should be an answer to his prayer.

Jesus was called "Master" in his time but he certainly was not the paradigm that would be adopted by today's "masters," whether presidents, generals, CEOs, bosses, employers, politicians, or businesspersons. He led by example and deliberately assumed the role of a servant at specific times to prove a point. Unlike today's barrage of messages that indoctrinate us into believing that we are the center of the universe, the emphasis of Jesus was to let everyone know that the least would be the greatest in the kingdom to come. Jesus transformed individuals not because he fooled them into believing that he could give them what they wanted, but because he persisted in giving people what they needed. We must react strongly to abuses of power that diminish the value of the individual. Today there are more slaves than during the peak time of formal slavery. There are women, girls, and boys who are in sexual captivity. There are millions of women and children whose sole value is no more than what they can produce economically, whether it is a product that can be sold or sexual exploitation. These forms of slavery exist because there are those who fail to see the value of individuals and because too many others are indifferent to how unfortunate people are valued. There are entire countries whose people live in poverty and sickness because their political leaders see themselves as having greater value than the individuals whom they promised to serve.

We can think of no better example than Jesus and the way in which he lived out the principle of valuing individuals no matter what their station in life. This was obvious even in his selection of his disciples.

THE DISCIPLES

The ministry of Jesus thrived on breaking down the barriers of position. From the beginning he chose his disciples from men of ordinary circumstance—men who had no wealth, who were likely to experience periods of unemployment. All the disciples except one came from Galilee, a region of Israel looked down upon by many. Today if we were to choose twelve individuals to whom we would entrust the future destiny of Christianity or our corporation or our country, we would certainly require detailed résumés from thousands of individuals from around the world. We would screen them by eliminating anyone who was poor, anyone who lacked political power, anyone who lacked an educational degree, and in all likelihood anyone who was not famous. The top twelve candidates would have names that would be widely recognized and whose biographies, recommendations, and aspirations were consistent with the correct social and political views of the day. We would want to hear them speak so that we could be assured they would not stumble over words, could present with confidence and have "charisma" to charm an audience. Individuals with the background and demeanor of the disciples would be the first ones eliminated. But they were chosen by Jesus, who knew their individual value. In no way were they ever invisible to him. Some of the followers of Jesus wanted to make him king, but his example was that of a servant. Because he went into the homes of people who were shunned by the establishment, he was shunned by the religious community and the leaders of the day. He washed his disciple's feet over their own objections. He rebuked them when they wanted to establish themselves in positions of importance. He chastised the disciples when they attempted to prevent children from sitting at his feet to listen to his teachings. He reached out to the poor. He healed the sick. He protected women who were condemned by the religious authorities. He overturned ideas about just wages. He called for justice, not rewards. He called for viewing others as equal in value.

Seeing value in an individual may mean investing in them economically as well as socially and spiritually. This may require breaking down economic and social disparities. Neither Jesus nor Paul sought to establish a political or economic system to solve what they perceived to be the fundamental needs of humankind in spite of the poverty and hunger that they dealt with on a daily basis. He met the needs of the crowds that followed him. Paul overturned a master-servant relationship that evolved into a deep personal relationship, saying, "I return him to you no longer as a slave but as a dear brother."

We cannot avoid dipping into some discussion of the use of resources, and also political systems that have risen and fallen through the years. Policies and systems eventually impact the man on the street or in the mud hut or the one without even a hut. The conversation reaches beyond our comfort zones.

LOSING THE WAY?

In our own lifetime we have seen many social, political, educational, and religious institutions that have lost their way. Economic systems have fostered investment schemes that devalue the precious resources of individuals and are then permitted to walk away from their failures without any obligation or guilt. Democracy, established to protect individuals and provide religious freedom, is threatened by those who use individual freedom to take advantage of the poor and powerless and those who hold strongly to religious. Capitalism, which brought economic freedom to hundreds of millions, threatens the poorest as world markets preserve personal profit over the welfare of the individual. Communism, heralded as the salvation of the masses, sacrificed the value of the individual, especially their spiritual value, and as a consequence collapsed, as individuals were valued solely for what they could contribute to the state. These and other systems have a common failure in that they begin with promises to protect the value of the individual only to slowly slip into bureaucracies where the value of the individual is lost. In summary, Christians in particular, when confronted with issues of justice and equity, must ask themselves two questions: "For what purpose have I achieved my position of power?" and, "Could it be that that the wealth I have achieved was not just for me but so others can have the same opportunities as I've had?"

MAYBE IT'S NOT FOR ME TO KEEP?

The test of our progress is not whether we add more to the abundance of those who have much; it is whether we provide enough for those who have too little.[8]

I was at a ski resort visiting the home of a wealthy corporate executive during the depth of an economic decline. The home was large and grand and everything in it seemed to have been specially made to emphasize its opulence. As I walked through the home I was cognizant that the owner's company had just laid off over five thousand workers. It was not his only home. It was one of three, and he only lived in this one for a month out of the year, during the peak of ski season. The remainder of the time he divided equally between two large homes in warmer climates. Curious, I prudently asked, how could all those people (there were hundreds of other homes of equal grandeur in the same area) afford these obviously expensive homes during a time of such severe economic stress? He quickly replied, "You have to put your money somewhere." His answer haunted me. Here was one person trying to find a place to park his wealth, while over five thousand people from the company that he oversaw, from which he had gained his wealth, were worrying about losing their only home along with their savings, their healthcare, their children's education, and their dreams. It never entered into his reasoning that perhaps his wealth was accumulated not for his sole use, but also for those who were now facing poverty.

I have often puzzled over the Bible story of the rich young ruler, where Jesus talks to an individual who, by all accounts, had accumulated his wealth in a highly ethical manner. We unpack the story that Jesus

8. Franklin D. Roosevelt, Second Inaugural Address, January 20, 1937, online: http://historyquotes.org/franklin-d-roosevelt-quotes/.

told about this young man and realize that its stinging message still applies today.

> Just then a man came up to Jesus and asked, "Teacher, what good thing must I do to get eternal life?"
>
> "Why do you ask me about what is good?" Jesus replied. "There is only One who is good. If you want to enter life, keep the commandments."
>
> "Which ones?" he inquired.
>
> Jesus replied, "'You shall not murder, you shall not commit adultery, you shall not steal, you shall not give false testimony, honor your father and mother,' and 'love your neighbor as yourself.'"
>
> "All these I have kept," the young man said. "What do I still lack?"
>
> Jesus answered, "If you want to be perfect, go, sell your possessions and give to the poor, and you will have treasure in heaven. Then come, follow me."
>
> When the young man heard this, he went away sad, because he had great wealth.
>
> Then Jesus said to his disciples, "Truly I tell you, it is hard for someone who is rich to enter the kingdom of heaven. Again I tell you, it is easier for a camel to go through the eye of a needle than for someone who is rich to enter the kingdom of God." (Matt 19:16–24)

Jesus extracts from the rich young man an acknowledgment that he has kept all the commandments. The rich man is not therefore a person who acquired his wealth through deceit or thievery. Nor is he a person who was so jealous of the wealth of others so that obtaining wealth became an obsession to outdo them. But Jesus pointed out that there was one thing that he lacked: "Go sell your possessions and give to the poor." There are many interpretations of this story. In the context of Jesus' teachings and Paul's in his letter to Philemon, the problem that Jesus saw was that the rich man did not pause to consider to whom his wealth belonged. His answer was immediate and defensive. But in reality what he possessed belonged to God—that was the point that Jesus was making without saying it. We too can be confused and rationalize our wealth as belonging solely to us. We can even give a lot away. But it is only when we acknowledge that it all belongs to God, that we are only a conduit for its distribution—it is only then that we see why we have been given so much. One problem with being successful and obtaining a position of great influence is that it too often results in the wrong sense of identity. A person can come to believe that they are the most important and indispensable beings in their universe and the one for whom everyone else exists. It has been termed by psychiatrists as "acquired narcissism" and it is precisely opposite of how Jesus viewed himself. He became the servant, the one who died for the least. Up until the last moment of death he was aware of the needs of one person when he said to the thief beside him, "Truly I tell you, today you will be with me in paradise" (Luke 23:43).

It is clear that Arthur has seen incredible examples of poverty in his career-related travels, and I have not, so I asked him to give some examples of equity and justice from his wide perspective.

It is difficult to not be judgmental of extreme wealth. Should we not, after all, celebrate it? For me it is a wrenching emotional adjustment as I travel from one resource-poor country to another where I am welcomed into unpainted clapboard homes by families of six or more living in one room without electricity or running water and only enough food for one meal each day, only to find myself, after one airplane ride and a short drive, among the excesses of wealth that surround me in the US. It is the issue of justice that overcomes me and I wonder, if we really stop to think about how we acquire wealth, wouldn't we need to acknowledge that we should not tolerate having such extremes of abundance and poverty? Wealth is relative. Many of us can feel poor when we enter the lavish surroundings of the rich. But there is also another form of wealth, one that takes what is less and reinterprets it as abundance. Jesus observed this and pointed it out to his disciples.

> As Jesus looked up, he saw the rich putting their gifts into the temple treasury. He also saw a poor widow put in two very small copper coins. "Truly I tell you," he said, "this poor widow has put in more than all the others. All these people gave their gifts out of their wealth; but she out of her poverty put in all she had to live on." (Luke 21:1–4)

With these words we are reminded that it often does not take much to make a profound difference, no matter what our status. But what of injustice? We often avoid this subject because of the guilt and discomfort we feel. It is really about the value of individuals and how easily injustice can be both the cause and the consequence of invisibility.

SUPPRESSING VISIBILITY

Many of us have experienced a moment when injustice becomes so clear that we should not turn our back on it. One such moment occurred during a National Institutes of Health–sponsored meeting on HIV vaccines. The international meeting brought together researchers from around the world to discuss the latest ideas and progress toward a vaccine that could halt the seemingly unstoppable onslaught of the worldwide HIV epidemic. In addition to professional researchers, the National Institutes of Health also paid the cost for community representatives from resource-poor countries—ordinary, perhaps invisible people, so to speak—to attend the meetings in the US. These representatives typically provided advice to HIV clinical research sites in their communities and offered insight into the real-world issues of HIV to the people who participate in the studies. Without them, few individuals would volunteer to be research subjects.

During this particular meeting a physician friend of mine noticed that one of the community representatives from South Africa seemed very ill. He took a risk and asked if he was on HIV treatment. He was stunned to hear the young man say that he was HIV infected but had no access to treatment in his own country. An immediate issue of justice emerged. Due to a bureaucratic tangle of regulations, a poor young HIV infected volunteer dedicated to helping HIV patients in vaccine studies could not afford the life-saving drugs that he himself so desperately needed, and no one was helping. Instead, despite his advanced illness, he was flown to an all-expense-paid US government meeting to help develop an AIDS vaccine. What would it have cost to save his life? Perhaps less than $100 a year—less than 3 percent of the cost of the airline ticket that brought him to the United States for the meeting, and perhaps no more than one dinner for two of the US researchers attending the meeting.

Deeply troubled by the experience, my physician friend returned to San Francisco and proceeded to contact the meeting participants asking if they would donate to pay for the young man's drugs. Only a few individuals were willing to contribute. The organizational replies came back not unsurprisingly as, "This is not the US government's responsibility; this is not the responsibility of researchers; if we started with one there will be no end to it; we would be distracted from our mission to develop an AIDS vaccine," and other excuses that smacked of the story of the Good Samaritan. Leaders in the US research effort suggested that the issue be pursued with the research site in South Africa while knowing that it was too poor to provide the medicine. The indifference was profound. Shortly after returning to South Africa the young man died, apparently from the complications of AIDS—a stinging indictment on the indifference of those who were using this sick community worker to facilitate access to research subjects but viewed him as of such little value that they could not act to overcome their irrational concerns. It was difficult to understand the arrogance of a group of scientists seeking to save the world from HIV by means of vaccine research while turning a blind eye to a real person in their midst whom they could have rescued from death for less than $100. Their rationale had made the person invisible and in the process denied the value of the one who was with them.

When Jesus told the story of the Good Samaritan he was not introducing socialism into the world nor was he illustrating the potential for capitalism to help humankind. He was pointing out that recognizing the value of an individual who enters into our sphere should cause us to take some of what we have, including time, compassion, and money, and invest it in the lives of the needy. Indifference to the value of a person happens all too easily. In a society that is infiltrated with materialism and gives homage to wealth, fame, and power, individuals who acquire these often come to believe that it is the sole result of their own abilities. They forget about the individuals who provided them with the labor, individuals who made their environment safe, workers who placed their savings in seemingly secure investments trusting that businesses and corporations who accepted their money would return it with greater value. They forget that all they have acquired was built and maintained by "ordinary" people.

> A person who pulls himself up from a low environment via the bootstrap route has two choices. Having risen above his environment, he can forget it; or, he can rise above it and never forget it and keep compassion and understanding in his heart for those he has left behind him in the cruel upclimb.[9]

The teachings of Jesus and Paul are clear. We must not allow centuries of time to erase them, individuals or organizations to reinterpret them, or to cause us to forget our own beginnings. Cultural, political, social, economic, and even religious distinctions that foster superior and inferior roles, whether based on power, wealth, education, social, ethnic, or even religious distinctions, must not devalue an individual. Those who find their value or identity in power, wealth, or fame without addressing issues of justice and equity are doomed to leave their own value undiscovered. The eventual impact will go beyond themselves. More than a master, Jesus viewed himself as a servant to set an example before us. Those in "high" positions must see the value of those "below" them. And those in "low" positions must see the value of those "above" them. But in all instances, it is the mutual recognition of the intrinsic value of each person that allows us to break down the barriers that cause dissensions, inequities, injustice, and even violence. "From everyone who has been given much, much will be demanded; and from the one who has been entrusted with much, much more will be asked." (Luke 12: 48)

THINK ON THESE THINGS

1. How does justice, a theme that runs throughout the Old and New Testaments, relate to the visibility and value of a person?

9. Betty Smith, *A Tree Grows in Brooklyn* (New York: Harper Collins, 1943), 147.

2. How does the impersonal trend and mass appeal of modern culture contribute to devaluation of individuals?

3. Was Jesus more sympathetic to the poor than to the wealthy? If so what might account for this difference?

4. How do issues of power, control, wealth, and mass appeal affect our understanding of the value of an individual?

6

Strangers and Angels

It is as none other than Paul—an old man and now also a prisoner of Christ Jesus—that I appeal to you for my son Onesimus, who became my son while I was in chains. Formerly he was useless to you, but now he has become useful both to you and to me. (Phlm 9–11)

Paul and Onesimus were strangers. The letter to Philemon brings into focus a provocative but mysterious concept as we attempt to understand and live out the meaning and purpose of our lives. How do we view strangers who are often nothing more than invisible individuals on the periphery of our lives? When they are thrust into our lives, often under unusual circumstances, are they diversions who keep us from our true purpose or are they angels that deliver messages to us to lead us into an uncharted journey of God's choosing?

Paul could have ignored the obscure runaway slave and have been perfectly justified in the eyes of many. He could have been indignant and resentful that his false imprisonment put him in the same prison as someone who was truly guilty of a crime. After all, Paul was highly educated, spoke multiple languages, was a citizen of multiple countries, and was regarded as a spiritual leader. Further, he was imprisoned for doing the work that

God had called him to do. With his importance and value to the emerging Christian community, he could have easily considered imprisonment as a waste of time. In advancing years, when time was short, he could have claimed that he needed to be about "God's work," ministering to thousands of individuals.

While in prison Paul could have compiled a long list of his "successes." Instead, he used his time to write letters to instruct, encourage, comfort, and on this occasion, to record, in the form of a very personal letter to a friend, the transformation of himself and a slave. The preservation of this letter was not without purpose. It takes us from the weighty matters of the emerging early church to the very foundational importance of the individual.

Through this snapshot of Paul, I see an image of our world today and the way we relate to strangers. The temptation is always present to disregard an intruding stranger as a detour, or at a minimum an annoying interruption, but we learn from Paul that a valuable relationships may be in store.

STRANGERS

I believe that we are increasingly becoming a culture of strangers, devoid of meaningful communication and often rejecting opportunities to interact with someone with unknown value to us—missing the potential to exchange life-directing experiences. We travel long distances on airplanes, sometimes for eight hours or more, with headphones over our ears signaling our wish for isolation. We sit and watch senseless advertisements that shout "Look at me!" while the person next to us quietly yearns for a few comforting words. We spend hours in front of computer screens reacting passively to what others tell us is important. The voices of teachers and students, once punctuated with revealing facial expressions and body movements, are gone, replaced by prerecorded "educational" material displayed on yet another computer monitor. We eliminate human voice, eye, and physical contact and are told that we are communicating and learning, all in the name of efficiency and progress.

Perhaps we need to get past the feelings of awkwardness and reticence about strangers and approach them as an opportunities rather than as obstacles.

More than ever I have observed how deep a conversation can go with a stranger if we are willing to go just one sentence past the perfunctory, "Hello, how are you?" There may be a risk of being taken advantage of by a stranger. Today the fear of that risk must diminish as the need for human interaction increases. There are few individuals who are willing to listen— to really listen to what someone has to say and to convey the message, "You are important and I want to hear more." If we, as individuals or a church, are to recover the essence of the ministry of Jesus, we must first seek out the individual in the crowd, the strangers, those who don't receive attention or are not in the spotlight of recognition. Jesus reached out to individuals who were invisible strangers to others—the child with the loaves and fishes, the woman who merely gave two copper pennies, the thief on the cross. We too must seek to find these people.

I believe Jesus tells us through his example that our concern is to be with individuals. We should not judge our ministry or the ministry of others based on numbers. Transformation is about the person, not about a religion or a political or economic system.

One word jumps out to me—transformation. In our culture it is much used with many different applications and various depths of meaning. It seems necessary to clarify the term for our discussion.

I believe that there is often an unconscious yearning to be transformed and to transform others. At a superficial level this may simply involve a discussion between two individuals with differing points of view in which one, or both, seek to persuade the other about a particular issue. At a deeper level it involves the engagement of spiritual values that seek to encourage a transformation of the inner being. The depth and duration of transformation may be variable, especially in a society inundated with superficialities and burdened with the intrusions of materialism. With strangers, it is necessary to break through the wall of unimportant demands that surround us in order to fully embrace the value of true spiritual transformation.

I am intrigued by the potential role of strangers in our lives. In order to understand another, I suspect it is important to see the other in their own context and surroundings. I think it would be helpful if somehow we could be transplanted to the other person's culture, unfamiliar to us, to extract ourselves from our own smothering reality. Perhaps we could then see the "invisible person" come into view and focus.

A JOURNEY OF STRANGERS TO JOS, NIGERIA

There could not have been a more unlikely group of strangers that gathered for a trip to a faith-based hospital and clinic in Jos, Nigeria. The purpose was to conduct a four-day workshop on HIV prevention and care for traditional birth attendants. With me were twelve volunteers. Our backgrounds varied—actor, movie director, bookstore owner, scientist, physician, writer, documentarian, insurance agent, decorator, pastor, and business executive.

All those on the journey agreed to abandon their occupation for a brief time in order to volunteer to help in the workshop training. All except one had never been to a resource-poor country. Immersion occurred quickly. Within an hour's drive from the Abuja airport the landscape changed precipitously and by evening we were completely immersed in surroundings that lacked the amenities of our culture.

During the time we had in Jos each of us lived and ate with families who were engaged in the HIV epidemic. We quickly learned that it was not their choice to become involved. It was an epidemic of great proportions that had descended on them and engulfed their daily lives.

We visited schools for HIV orphans, spoke to HIV widows, met sexually abused young girls, and met with families that had been devastated by the premature deaths of mothers, fathers, and children. As we immersed ourselves in the pain that we saw and felt, we began to hold hands, sing songs composed by those infected with HIV, and listen to words that spoke of suffering and hope. All of us were meeting strangers who were allowing us to enter into their lives and, in doing so, they also entered into ours, helping us to learn about their suffering and pain.

Later, one of the volunteers, a movie director, expressed it this way: "I search for the meaningful. When I am at work, I manage people and tell them what to do and where to go and I am good at it. Here, I listen to people that I can't manage. I'm just here to listen to them and to help them." More than once I saw her overwhelmed with emotion as individuals, who she had never before met, came up to her and expressed their gratefulness. She went to help and to touch someone in need but found that she herself had been embraced with spiritual healing and transformation.

On the last day of the workshop we had a closing ceremony, a sort of graduation. As the birth attendants expressed their gratitude to us for coming to help them, I looked around the room and saw the tears streaming down the faces of many of the volunteers who had come to help. The birth attendants who had come from the rural areas outside of Jos, and the HIV-infected men, women, and children whose existence was not previously known to the volunteers, were no longer strangers but were transformed into people with faces, names, and stories.

Later that day I saw members of our group embrace their host families trying to hold back tears as they said farewell. We made our way to the airport, retracing those first initial steps of uncertainty, realizing that we might never see some of these people again. They began as strangers but had now become visible and their memories would forever linger to transform how we viewed HIV and the pain and suffering that these people had to endure.

What happened during those days? There was transformation of individuals. The HIV epidemic was no longer just a fact or an amorphous mass of over twenty-five million HIV-infected individuals worldwide. It had become about a real person who stood by you, held your hand, and prayed for healing. It was a mother who could be touched and who expressed herself in tears or song. It was a child who struggled to breathe even while sitting still. It was a father who lost his job because of the stigma of HIV, and with it all of the financial support for his family. It was a man dying of AIDS with his wife beside him, with no hope for treatment and a doctor saying, "Your hope must be in God."

The transformation of these individuals was brought about by direct engagement. It was no longer "those people over there." It was now about

Esther, Samuel, Hope, Precious—people whose names we learned but whose names Jesus had known all along. He had walked with them, hand in hand, and now they joined hands with us to begin a new journey.

What I felt at the end of our time in Jos is difficult to put into words but it seemed that in reaching out to a person, not with money or promises or solutions, but with compassion, we were all able to reach deeply into the treasures of God's resources, and receive the reward of spiritual abundance. The teachings of Jesus became clear, "Truly I tell you, whatever you did for one of the least of these brothers and sisters of mine, you did for me" (Matt 25:40). God knows no strangers. He knows their faces, their names; he feels their every need, and from time to time he provides us with the opportunity and the privilege of meeting them and knowing them as he does.

Another African example surfaces. Although there is a chasm between the distant worlds of Jos, Nigeria, and Cape Town, South Africa, it is the same God who transcends continents and oceans to speak into our lives about how we should view and treat strangers

THE WIDOW'S HOME

Strangers may also bring us into their world and even go so far as welcoming us into their home to teach us lessons that cannot be learned unless we experience them with all of our senses. It is often insufficient to simply hear the words or imagine the vision. One such experience stands out in my mind as we found ourselves in South Africa in the middle of a township, a term for what we could call a slum. It was as appalling as anything I had seen in photographs. The contrast of this slum to the well-appointed modern international airport in Cape Town made it seem even more poverty stricken. I was with a pastor and his wife, both born in South Africa. They were from a church in Cape Town that had never visited a township to see firsthand what they knew intellectually was there. They were good people. Every Sunday they put a plate of their best china outside their front door, covered with food, for some beggar who might wander through their neighborhood. But they were overwhelmed with the poverty that they saw in the township and somewhat embarrassed that it took an American to take them to see what they had lived so close to for their entire lives.

(in)Visible

My memory of that visit is mostly about an elderly woman, Philippa, a widow who had struggled to survive for decades. We were strangers to her and she to us, but she trusted us to see the fulfillment of her dream of an entire lifetime.

A program for widows had been established in the township and it provided Philippa with training skills to earn her first income in years. She carefully saved what she could until there was enough to buy a small plot of land on which she built a home consisting of remnants of wood, cardboard, and corrugated metal. She desperately wanted us, visitors from America, to see her home. Arm and arm we walked down the middle of one of the dirt roads in the township, past homes that qualified for the term only because there were people living inside, until we came to her home. We were invited in. The five of us just barely fit in comfortably, without spilling outside the one doorway. Standing in one location we could almost touch all the furniture on the periphery of the room without moving—an armchair, a single table with two chairs, a place to cook, a bed.

Once we were assembled, she stood in the middle of the room, looked at us, and announced, "This is my home, and God gave it to me." This widow of poverty had proudly invited us into her home to share what God given her. There was an innocence and yet great sense of pride in what we, in all likelihood, would have been embarrassed for others to see.

On the long flight home through London and then to San Francisco I thought frequently of the grand homes that I had visited in the US— from Beverly Hills to Beaver Creek and to Manhattan—homes that were guarded and gated, immense, grand, and inviting. Yet no strangers were invited into these homes to share what God had given. Philippa, a stranger in a township in South Africa, with so little in our materialistic eyes, not only invited us as strangers into her home, but thanked God for what he had given to her to share with us.

We live in all kinds of gated communities. The wealth and spaciousness of many homes is reserved for the few individuals of like circumstances. Those who live under poorer circumstances pass on the outside. Perhaps we also live in spiritually gated communities, keeping strangers outside our hearts and minds, never going beyond the perfunctory "hello," closing all opportunities to meet that individual who just might have a transforming influence over us.

In our lives we may not encounter just one stranger at a time, but many all at once. Their needs may overwhelm us. It happened to me on my first trip to India. I had been there for no more than several days when I began to feel certain hopelessness.

ENCOUNTER IN INDIA

I had been invited to give the opening ceremony address at one of the first international conferences on HIV in India. India, more than any other country, seemed too overwhelming with its population of over one billion people, its poverty, its diversity of religions and languages.

I was sitting in front of a hotel window in Chennai, reading my New Testament and gazing out to the masses of people gathering on the street, and thinking, "What can I say to these people who are beginning to experience the impact of a major epidemic?" Then I read these words:

> When Jesus came down from the mountainside, large crowds followed him. A man with leprosy came and knelt before him and said, "Lord, if you are willing, you can make me clean."
> Jesus reached out his hand and touched the man. "I am willing," he said. "Be clean!" Immediately he was cleansed of his leprosy. (Matt 8:1–3)

The story of Jesus and the leper provided the clarity that I needed. Jesus reached out to heal that one leper who came to him. Previously, the leper was a stranger to Jesus. There must have been thousands of lepers in Jerusalem and the surrounding regions, but at that moment in time he devoted his attention to just one person.

In my opening address, I posed the question, "Where do we begin when we are faced with a seemingly overwhelming epidemic of thousands of people? We begin by meeting the needs of that one person, even a person who has been made invisible through a disease like AIDS, and we do it without fear and without discrimination.

ॐ

It is easy to lose our focus on an individual when we are all awash in information and news. The constant intrusion of world problems and cries that we must mobilize to solve them too often leave us overwhelmed. It may seem that there is too much to be done or that the forces of evil are too powerful. We are told in Scripture, "Do not be overcome by evil but overcome evil with good." We should not be overcome by the needs of the world but rather we are to address the singular needs of those who enter our sphere of influence. Jesus' teaching was clear: "[W]hatever you did for one of the least of these brothers and sisters of mine, you did for me" (Matt 25:40).

With all these examples regarding strangers, it occurs to me that our conversation began with reference not only to strangers but also to angels. This part of the equation seems more difficult to wrap my arms around. I am out of my experiential element at this point.

I am not certain what to make of angels either—whether they are just strangers with a message to advise us or if they really come to our side to protect and direct us. I certainly have not seen an angel as depicted by the old masters or described by those who have seen visions of them. During a near-death experience that I had, the moments "out there" were so vivid that I experienced "peace beyond understanding." I still long for those moments today, but there were no angels present during that experience.

Angels are described as interveners who provide direction and remove fear of change. Many writers are convinced of their existence and write in vivid detail of their presence. The Danish poet Pia Northrup wrote, "An angel came in—we fled from him as though we had got too near the fire." The modern Irish writer Lorna Byrne, who wrote *Angels in My Hair*, was convinced of the personal nature of angels. Both the Old and the New Testaments describe angels that directed prophets such as Moses and Gideon, but also appeared to ordinary people such as Hagar, Zachariah, Elizabeth, Mary, and Joseph. Without the appearance of angels they might not have believed and realized their destinies.

A STRANGER ON THE STREET—OR WAS HE AN ANGEL?

It was a cold winter day in New York City. My wife, Marilyn, and I with our friend Susan were on our way to the theater. We had decided to walk rather than risk our lives in a Manhattan taxi. Besides, during the peak of traffic congestion it was often faster to walk.

We were skillfully avoiding as many people as possible while trying to stay together. As we were crossing Park Avenue, integrated into a streaming mass of people, I saw a figure coming directly toward me. He was bobbing up and down, more so than others, as if in another world. As he approached I could hear him chant, "Help me, help me, help me." The chant increased in volume as he brushed past me. I felt his physical contact on my arm. There was no eye contact and he never stopped to speak to anyone in spite of his plea. When I reached the other side of the street, I turned around and saw him disappear into the blur of the moving crowd.

It is likely that under most circumstances, a stranger in New York City chanting "Help me" would elicit only a momentary impression and would be quickly forgotten. But the next day, the next week, and for the next several months his chant played through my mind day and night. I was in New York during a transition time in my career and seeking what God wanted me to do next. I had agreed to be president of the American Foundation for AIDS Research for a year to assist them with prioritizing their research programs. They were headquartered in Manhattan and although I had been raised in Brooklyn I had no desire to return to New York City permanently, and so my wife and I agreed to a one-year term, living in an apartment for one week each month and returning to our home in California for the remaining three weeks each month.

To some the circumstances might have seemed ideal—the best of New York and the best of California, jetting across country, to experience the contrast of cultures and geography. But it was an interlude during which I wrestled with what God wanted me to do next.

What had been weighing heavily on me was the issue of justice. I had seen the medical advances in the HIV epidemic in the US reduce the number of HIV-infected children from thousands each year to less than one hundred. At the same time I knew that the numbers of children infected each year in resource-poor countries was eight thousand times greater. I also knew that it would take very little money to take medical advances to the poor in the countries that were most affected by the HIV epidemic.

I had been given the financial means to begin a non-profit foundation but I needed a "voice" to push me into a decision. To this day, fifteen years after our foundation started, I don't know if that voice was a chance encounter with a stranger or the voice of an angel instructing me to heed the voices of those in great need.

It seems that strangers and angels may conspire to transform an individual. We read of this in the New Testament in the book of Acts. Philip the evangelist was very specifically directed by an angel to meet an unlikely stranger, an Ethiopian eunuch.

> Now an angel of the Lord said to Philip, "Go south to the road—the desert road—that goes down from Jerusalem to Gaza." So he started out, and on his way he met an Ethiopian eunuch, an important official in charge of all the treasury of the Kandake (which means "queen of the Ethiopians"). This man had gone to Jerusalem to worship, and on his way home was sitting in his chariot reading the Book of Isaiah the prophet. The Spirit told Philip, "Go to that chariot and stay near it."
>
> Then Philip ran up to the chariot and heard the man reading Isaiah the prophet. "Do you understand what you are reading?" Philip asked.
>
> "How can I," he said, "unless someone explains it to me?" So he invited Philip to come up and sit with him.
>
> This is the passage of Scripture the eunuch was reading:
> "He was led like a sheep to the slaughter,
> and as a lamb before its shearer is silent,
> so he did not open his mouth.
> In his humiliation he was deprived of justice.
> Who can speak of his descendants?
> For his life was taken from the earth."
>
> The eunuch asked Philip, "Tell me, please, who is the prophet talking about, himself or someone else?" Then Philip began with that very passage of Scripture and told him the good news about Jesus.

As they traveled along the road, they came to some water and the eunuch said, "Look, here is water. What can stand in the way of my being baptized?" And he gave orders to stop the chariot. Then both Philip and the eunuch went down into the water and Philip baptized him. When they came up out of the water, the Spirit of the Lord suddenly took Philip away, and the eunuch did not see him again, but went on his way rejoicing. (Acts 8:26–39)

Brief encounters with strangers or angels initiate the process of transformation. The Gospels tells the story of Jesus pressing through the crowd. Suddenly he asks, "Who touched me?" His followers were skeptical that anyone in particular had touched him other than the normal press of the crowd. But the woman and Jesus both knew that they had touched one another and in those brief seconds spiritual and physical transformation had occurred. I believe we're told this story because God wants us to know that his revelations to us may be so seemingly trivial that they risk being overlooked.

Angels have played an important and recurring role throughout both the Old and New Testaments. Many books and first-person stories of people who have encountered angel intervention circulate in our modern times. Here lies another mystery of faith that is up to each person to embrace or not. Regardless of our individual conclusion about angels, we will all unmistakably encounter many strangers in our lifetime. Leaving our doors open to welcome strangers with love might well allow the unexpected opportunity to entertain "angels unaware." Scripture instructs us, " Do not forget to show hospitality to strangers, for by so doing some people have shown hospitality to angels without knowing it" (Heb 13:2).

THINK ON THESE THINGS

1. What traits or appearances of a stranger cause them to remain invisible to you? (Such as tattoos, piercings, physical deformities or extreme obesity.)

2. Has there been a stranger or an unanticipated individual who has become very important to you personally? How did this come about? How do you interpret it in the context of your own life's journey?

3. What are your beliefs regarding the link between strangers and angels? What are your beliefs regarding the possible reality of angels interacting with people?

7

The Mystery of One

*Therefore, although in Christ I could be bold and order you to do what
you ought to do, yet I appeal to you on the basis of love. It is as none other
than Paul—an old man and now also a prisoner of Christ Jesus—that
I appeal to you for my son Onesimus, who became my son while I was
in chains. Formerly he was useless to you, but now he has become useful
both to you and to me.* (Phlm 8–11)

Our conversation to this point reminds me of the journey through life—
as if we were weaving threads into a single fabric, rich in texture and
color. The warp and woof of particular relationships—friends, siblings,
children, spouses—combine into a visible result, discovering a person of value. We attempt to bring it all together into a summary, an
equation or a report of sorts. However, a yet unspoken suggestion of
mystery still hangs in the air. Arthur offers a quote from an ancient and
admired priest and poet, John Donne, and it catapults us headlong
into yet another interesting, but puzzling discussion.

> All mankind is of one author, and is one volume; when
> one man dies, one chapter is not torn out of the book,

> but translated into a better language; and every chapter
> must be so translated. . . . As therefore the bell that rings
> to a sermon, calls not upon the preacher only, but upon
> the congregation to come: so this bell calls us all: but how
> much more me, who am brought so near the door by
> this sickness. . . . No man is an island, entire of itself . . .
> any man's death diminishes me, because I am involved in
> mankind; and therefore, never send to know for whom
> the bell tolls; it tolls for thee.[10]

My thoughts are often entwined with the mystery of the essential value of one person and our purpose in relation to a single individual. Is it possible for example, that our entire life—everything that we thought was important in our own spiritual journey, our varied ministries, our public service, our occupation, the relationships we have built, our education, and our professional development—might just have been a series of stepping stones in the pathway to meet just one individual of great value—an individual to be transformed, or who will transform us, as a result of our mutual encounter? In the mystery of God's plans for his creation and where we fit in, could it possibly be that all we have previously experienced is merely a prelude to the one person who we are yet to meet? On occasions when I have presented this provocative thought to someone or to some group, it is invariably met with the response, "That can't be possible! There have been too many important people in my life with whom I have formed deep relationships. They have all been important. It can't be about just one person." But this concept that all that precedes us could be for one person, one moment in time that may direct our entire life, was catapulted into our imagination with the national news coverage of the US Airway crash on the Hudson River. On Friday, January 16, 2009, Captain Chesley "Sully" Sullenberger, a fifty-seven-year-old former Air Force fighter pilot, calmly brought his plane and the 155 passengers aboard to safety in a powerless aircraft, landing on New York's Hudson River, sandwiched between two major metropolitan areas. Sullenberger had forty years of aviation experience, about 20,000 flight hours in jets, propeller planes, and gliders, taught

10. John Donne, Meditation XVII, in John Booty, ed., *John Donne: Selections from Divine Poems, Sermons, Devotions, and Prayers* (New York: Paulist, 1990), 271–72.

emergency landings and prepared himself and other pilots for circumstances that neither he nor others thought would ever happen. In a television interview on *60 Minutes* he was asked, "What do you think about the entire event." He replied, "As I think about it, I believe my entire life was in preparation for that moment."

"The mystery of one," as I have named it in my own mind, conveys a sacredness about how we view the value of each person we encounter and the moments that we spend with them; that one person may be a stranger, a friend, a spouse, a sibling, a son or daughter, but that person is so significant that they cannot be overlooked in the complexity of the world we live in. No human can be discarded as incidental to the universe. In fact, even a moment in time with a given person can change the trajectory of a life, or both lives! What Donne, a poet and priest, wrestled with was the value of a single life—so precious, so important, that it could not simply disappear into the vapor of the universe. Another example is found in the Gospel of Luke. Mary and Joseph encounter Simeon, a man who had waited his entire life for a singular event, his meeting with the Messiah. When that meeting occurred, it was sufficient for him to utter, "Now I can die in peace."

> Now there was a man in Jerusalem called Simeon, who was righteous and devout. He was waiting for the consolation of Israel, and the Holy Spirit was on him. It had been revealed to him by the Holy Spirit that he would not die before he had seen the Lord's Messiah. Moved by the Spirit, he went into the temple courts. When the parents brought in the child Jesus to do for him what the custom of the Law required, Simeon took him in his arms and praised God, saying:
> "Sovereign Lord, as you have promised,
> you may now dismiss your servant in peace.
> For my eyes have seen your salvation,
> which you have prepared in the sight of all nations:
> a light for revelation to the Gentiles,
> and the glory of your people Israel." (Luke 2:25–32)

This is all that we are told about Simeon—nothing of his life before or after this single event. We are left with the impression that this might have been Simeon's sole purpose—to embrace the child Jesus, announce the Messiah, and confirm to Mary and Joseph their purpose. In this brief and momentary encounter, all of the participants were indelibly imprinted by the child Jesus. Decades later Jesus would begin his ministry. Although his ministry was confined to three brief years, he too would focus on seemingly singular events involving just one person.

I have noticed the same thing. At this point, it may be helpful to look at some of the specific encounters Jesus had with one person.

Reading about the life of Jesus, we cannot conclude that one person was more important than another. When Jesus was in a crowd, he often focused on a single obscure individual with a specific need—the woman with a bleeding disorder who touched him as others pressed to get closer, Zacchaeus the tax collector, who resorted to climbing a tree to get a glimpse of him, the crippled man lowered down through the roof by his friends, the man blind from birth. Jesus focused on individuals and often avoided crowds. It seemed as if crowds were trying to tempt him to divert his focus from individuals to becoming a powerful leader and king. Many wanted Jesus for the wrong reason.

It is also curious to observe how Jesus met with one person alone and transmitted to them foundational teachings that were to become pillars of Christian theology. Two of these individuals, Nicodemus and the Samaritan woman at a well, were not even known to be followers of Jesus and yet he valued them so highly that he entrusted them with spiritual truths not even shared with his disciples. Nicodemus sought Jesus covertly. His concern about being seen with the controversial teacher resulted in a secretive meeting at night. In spite of his hesitation, Jesus was prepared to reveal new spiritual truths to this man. Jesus went out of his way to meet him, to answer his questions, and in the process took him to a deeper level of personal introspection and spirituality with the words, "You must be born again." With those words, Jesus began a cascade of thoughts that would lead Nicodemus to understand that physical life is not the end; there is a fuller, deeper spiritual life ahead that takes a person beyond death. Few Christians realize that one of the most quoted verses of the Bible was spoken only to Nicodemus during that late evening meeting with no one else listening. "For God so loved the world that he gave his one and only Son, that whoever believes in him shall not perish but have eternal life" (John

3:16). It was a moment in time when Jesus imparted transforming truths to a single person, alone, and at night, cutting through the darkness of human understanding to communicate eternal truth.

Similarly, when Jesus met the Samaritan woman alone at a well, she was transformed as he told her about the living water he could offer her which would forever quench her thirst. Jesus did not allow the woman's questionable past to alter the depth of the spiritual truths that he shared with her. He did not dismiss her as invisible. In contrast, when the disciples returned they saw no value in her and expressed surprise that Jesus had met with this woman alone—a woman with multiple husbands, a Samaritan practicing what Jews considered to be a defective religion. The disciples avoided the spiritual opportunity of that encounter and instead focused on the physical as they sought food in the village.

> Just then his disciples returned and were surprised to find him talking with a woman. But no one asked, "What do you want?" or "Why are you talking with her?"
>
> Then, leaving her water jar, the woman went back to the town and said to the people, "Come, see a man who told me everything I ever did. Could this be the Messiah?" They came out of the town and made their way toward him.
>
> Meanwhile his disciples urged him, "Rabbi, eat something."
>
> But he said to them, "I have food to eat that you know nothing about."
>
> Then his disciples said to each other, "Could someone have brought him food?"
>
> "My food," said Jesus, "is to do the will of him who sent me and to finish his work. (John 4:27–34)

We see that something extraordinary happened here. Jesus explained food beyond the physical level which pre-occupied his disciples. There is food for thought, food for the soul, and as Jesus said here, "my food is to do the will of him who sent me . . ." This one-on-one meeting with a woman who was invisible to the disciples had significant purpose and outcomes. It was orchestrated by the will of God, and touched the lives of town's people and many readers through the ages, as well as the woman herself.

It is an intriguing story. In a mysterious way, Jesus himself was fed by this interaction, offering the woman at the well living water. When we choose to shut out an individual from our lives, as the disciples did with the woman, whether a stranger or a person who we may find fault with, we shut out the potential for us to transform one another. When an organization or a church chooses to close its doors to people who suffer spiritual or physical pain because they don't fit in or they don't have time, they lose their potential for the transformation of those individuals. When politics, religion, nationality, tribe, gender, or a disease like HIV determines whom we deem valuable, we abandon those in whom God is most interested. Jesus' story of the shepherd and the lost sheep is a reminder of encounters with just one person. In this story Jesus teaches us that one individual may be so valuable that we may appear to abandon those who surround us just to rescue one "lost" person.

> Then Jesus told them this parable: "Suppose one of you has a hundred sheep and loses one of them. Doesn't he leave the ninety-nine in the open country and go after the lost sheep until he finds it? And when he finds it, he joyfully puts it on his shoulders and goes home. Then he calls his friends and neighbors together and says, 'Rejoice with me; I have found my lost sheep.' I tell you that in the same way there will be more rejoicing in heaven over one sinner who repents than over ninety-nine righteous persons who do not need to repent. (Luke 15:3–7)

When Jesus told the story of the lost sheep it was not just about leaving the entire flock. It was about the value of one individual, a value that Jesus also saw in the very last moments of physical and spiritual pain at the time of his crucifixion. With only moments left in his own life and in spite of the extraordinary meaning of his own death, Jesus took the time to reply, "Today you will be with me in paradise."

> One of the criminals who hung there hurled insults at him: "Aren't you the Messiah? Save yourself and us!"

But the other criminal rebuked him. "Don't you fear God," he said, "since you are under the same sentence? We are punished justly, for we are getting what our deeds deserve. But this man has done nothing wrong."

Then he said, "Jesus, remember me when you come into your kingdom."

Jesus answered him, "Truly I tell you, today you will be with me in paradise." (Luke 23:39–43)

We agree that throughout his ministry Jesus teaches the importance of relationships above all else. He has no mathematical formula that counts the value of a crowd to be greater than that of an individual, or the feeding of five thousand a greater event than meeting quietly with an obscure individual who touched the hem of his robe, or that establishing a new movement or religion is more important than answering the question of one curious rabbi. As we attempt to apply this in our own lives, we sense the tension that exists between mass ministry and one-on-one contact.

Paul judged Onesimus as the most important person in his life at the time he was in prison, so much so as to call him his son. We are to recognize the person we encounter at any moment, as valuable.

Pope Benedict, in his book *Jesus of Nazareth*, wrote about why the individual must not be devalued and why a relationship with God must be maintained if we desire to achieve great things.

The aid offered by the West to developing countries has been purely technically and materially based, and not only has it left God out of the picture, but has driven men away from God. And this aid, proudly claiming to "know better," is its self what first turned the "third world" into what we mean today by that term. It has thrust aside indigenous religions, ethical, and social structures and filled the resulting vacuum with its technocratic mind set. The idea was that we could turn stones into bread, instead, our "aid" has only given stones in place of bread. The issue is the primacy of God. The issue is acknowledging that he is a reality, that he is the reality without which nothing else can be good. History cannot be detached

> from God and then run smoothly on purely material lines. If man's heart is not good then nothing else can turn out good, either. And the goodness of the human heart can only come from the One who is goodness, who is the Good itself.[11]

I would add that if we attempt to transform poverty or hunger by introducing some sort of a solely political or economic system without recognizing the value of the person who needs assistance, then our assistance is ultimately doomed to failure. But if we recognize their value, then they too will see value in one another and a chain reaction occurs. Each of us has a potential deep within us to find value in the unlikely person, as we acknowledge that we are all made in the image of God. It is not necessary to take special courses, watch instructional DVDs, listen to motivational speakers, attend seminars on personal development, or even read "how to" books. Jesus taught his disciples and us that we all have the tools to partner with God in the transformation of an individual. And because we participate, we receive the spiritual blessing he promised—which results in our own transformation as well. "Truly I tell you, whatever you did for one of the least of these brothers and sisters of mine, you did for me" (Matt 25:40). It is between God, us, and the person in need. Period!

We meet people every day whose value is worthy of being discovered. We must be sure we do not bypass them as being invisible. Like Philemon, we can easily miss a person of value. He was so preoccupied with his church its growth that he ignored one person within his own reach who was in great need. Onesimus was perhaps viewed as a person "below" Philemon's standing who could offer nothing to Philemon. Perhaps Philemon focused on wealthy individuals or individuals of great community standing or political importance. And so it was for Paul, far away in prison, to be given the privilege and the blessing of discovering this person of great importance to God, returning him to Philemon no longer as a slave but as a person of value—as he should have been viewed in the first place. In the end Onesimus was a person like so many whom Jesus focused on—those of lesser importance in society, obscure in the midst of religious activity

---

11. Pope Benedict XVI, *Jesus of Nazareth: From the Baptism in the Jordan to the Transfiguration* (San Francisco: Ignatius, 2007) 33–34.

and yet in great need of having their inner value recognized. Jesus ignored those who wanted to make him king, those who misinterpreted the power of his teaching to mean gaining political control. He reprimanded the disciples when they sought to develop some sort of hierarchy of who was most important. If we are to understand the enduring influence of the teachings of Jesus, we must understand how his message was so closely associated with the ultimate significance of a solitary man, woman, or child, and not organizations, religions, or political movements. He taught his followers to make value judgments based on personal relationships and not on popularity or majority opinion.

We keep returning to the words "mystery of one." This seems upstream in the light of today's constant emphasis on mass appeal, but we press on to understand the principles of the idea. We seek some link to help apply this to our lives today.

IT'S NOT ABOUT NUMBERS

The "mystery of one" is counter to our current culture and perhaps counter to some of our most closely held traditional cultural and religious teachings. We are indoctrinated with suggestions that all influence and importance are related to numbers. We evaluate the success of a new website by the number of "hits" and imply that these numbers reflect importance or relevance. Television programs survive or fail on the basis of Nielsen ratings, as if attention determines value. Advertisers follow newspaper and magazine circulation to determine how much they will spend on promoting a product. The world's countries are ranked in importance using economic figures, suggesting that these are the most important variables in determining greatness or the quality of life within countries. Professors at prestigious colleges and universities are judged by the number of publications they produce or the number of times their publications are cited. Universities are considered to be successful if the number of students enrolled increases each year or their campuses undergo continuous building programs to accommodate a multiplicity of relevant or even nonrelevant programs. Political influence is determined by wealth and power. A prestigious position is one that pays the highest salary or has the greatest visibility. Professional success is judged by the size of the home, the cost of the car, or the possession of luxuries. Even in religious communities success may be viewed as the number of individuals who attend a church, the number of churches that have been spawned, the number of programs that have been initiated, the number of prominent speakers, the number of viewers on television. We are told that bigger is better for everyone and everything.

We must be careful how far we deviate from Jesus' views on the importance of a single individual created in the image of God. We should not try to improve on his teachings, experimenting with new methods, heaping on ourselves and others knowledge without understanding, departing from relevance, always moving on to "new things" while leaving behind the value of the one person and trading it for the world's markers of success.

> The Eagle soars in the summit of Heaven,
> The Hunter with his dogs pursues his circuit.
> O perpetual revolution of configured stars,
> Oh world of spring and autumn, birth and dying!
> The endless cycle of idea and action,
> Endless invention, endless experiment,
> Brings knowledge of motion, but not of stillness;
> Knowledge of speech, but not of silence;
> Knowledge of words, and ignorance of the Word.
> All our knowledge brings us nearer to our ignorance,
> All our ignorance brings us near to death,
> But nearness to death no nearer to God.
> Where is the Life we have lost in living?
> Where is the knowledge we have lost in information?
> The cycles of Heaven in twenty centuries
> Bring us farther from God and nearer to the Dust.[12]

The church in America spends too much time and money trying convince millions of people of their need of God while actually ignoring the individual in need who is already in their midst or just outside their walls. They do this using every modern technique to capture the attention of the crowds, not realizing that they are using the same techniques that lured individuals

---

12. T. S. Eliot, opening stanza from "Choruses from 'The Rock,'" in *Selected Poems*, Centenary Edition, 1888–1988 (San Diego: Harcourt Brace, 1988), 107.

away from God in the first place. It is an escape from an intimate and personal relationship with the living God into dealing with numbers.

Reversing such a trend would be an enormous endeavor. But perhaps a simple shift in focus from mass appeal to discovering the value individual is all that is needed. In a recent book about spiritual transformation, Mindy Calaguire writes of leadership skills.

> They are wonderful skills that help people grow and are key tools in the process of spiritual formation. But skills and tools won't matter if there isn't a fundamental caring—a passionate desire to see God at work in just one person. When one person takes an authentic interest in someone else, qualities like discernment, direction and prayer move from being mechanical steps for successful leadership to behaviors that naturally characterize our relationships.[13]

Although we cannot change whole cultural systems, we can begin in our own sphere of influence, and our own behavior.

There are millions of people who experience pain and suffering who require only a few words of comfort from us to find the Great Comforter. As these individuals enter our sphere of living they can be transformed simply by being accepted as a person of value and deserving of our individual attention. We live in an age where technology has placed a chasm of abbreviated and impersonal communication between individuals. Yet God provides us with the capacity to usher an individual who is depressed, discouraged, or wounded into a transforming relationship with him. We can assure them that they are persons and not mere commodities. We can listen, touch, cry, and provide compassion, all of which are our God-given potentials. It is not something that needs to be purchased or needs to wait for some new technology to be developed. No computer, no cell phone, no text message, no email can substitute for what is already within us—the ability to see the value of a person and impart that assurance to them.

13. Mindy Caliguire, *Stir: Spiritual Transformation in Relationships* (Grand Rapids: Zondervan, 2013), 147.

We are smitten with the reality of our own responsibility as we interact with others. A good start is to increase "face time" rather than "screen time"—one-on-one contact, involving the heart as well as the head. We begin to explore existing obstacles to achieving personal interaction.

OBSTACLES

Our unwillingness to step out and to recognize those who are in need of transformation relates to our own discomfort and insecurity. In the practice of medicine it is considered malpractice to withhold healing. This is about acknowledging someone, conveying their value, and leaving them better for having been with us. It is about not withholding the power to recognize someone as valuable, whether in a brief encounter or an enduring relationship. It is what we see in the life of Jesus—an encounter that begins by recognizing the value of a person. Transformation is in the hands of a God who watches over every person as they journey through life. He brings two together by his divine appointment and offers the potential of a whole new way of life. We, however, want our lives to be judged as successful based on a long list of achievements and so we try hard to orchestrate everything in our lives—where we go, who we meet, where we live, what we do. We struggle with the right place to live, the best job, the best school for our children. We want people to know who we are so we put our personal photos and stories on Internet sites like YouTube and Facebook and Instagram. It is true that Paul tells us in Ephesians that God has prepared for each of us the good works that he wants us to perform. But it is also true that everything we do—including the good works of giving, meeting the needs of friends, caring for our family, helping the widows and orphans—is a process that might ultimately lead us to one last transforming relationship, to bring us to the purpose for which all else in our life exists.

We agree in theory but search for a specific life experience to flesh out the principle. Arthur relays a story of an remarkable relationship he easily could have missed.

JOSEPH CIZA—A NURSE WITH COMPASSION

It was my second visit to Goma, Congo. The year before I was introduced to the instability that plagues this region of Eastern Congo and had given it the reputation of being the worst region in Africa, for brutal violence and rape against women. There is no adequate explanation for the ongoing violence, which seems to be a continuation of the genocide in Rwanda. It is now being rehearsed again in the forests of the Congo. On this occasion I was there to conduct a workshop on HIV and AIDS, teaching healthcare workers how to prevent HIV, including infection of women and their babies and young girls following rape. I was told during the conference that I must meet Joseph Ciza. Somewhere in the middle of the conference I finally met Joseph. He came up to me and said simply, "I am Joseph Ciza."

Joseph walked with a limp as a result of a fracture in his leg that he suffered as a child and that was never properly set. He was short in stature and bore a facial expression that seemed to be a map of all of the suffering of Eastern Congo. When I said, "Joseph, I was told that I should meet you and find out more about you," he replied, "Do you want to know about me or do you want to know what I do?"

For a moment I was silenced. I had never had anyone ask me that question but I soon learned that his blunt but insightful inquiries are typical of him. Ciza, as he was often called, was about to take me on an unusual journey. Joseph rarely smiled when I spoke to him. He seemed to be surrounded with all of the seriousness of a man who had experienced too much of the world's suffering. But on some occasions he would laugh out loud. At first I thought that this laughter was inappropriate as it was often coupled with stories of tragedies and violence. But I soon realized that the momentary laughter was a means of overcoming the painful memories and deep scars that could not be overcome with tears. In 1996, two years after the Rwandan genocide, Joseph, a male nurse, found himself working alongside two American physicians trying to repair the damage inflicted by the unforgiving machetes of the Interahamwe who severed innocent human bodies into pieces—men, women, infants, elderly persons. I'm certain that after the genocide Joseph left Rwanda with emotional wounds, which, unlike the ones he helped to heal, repeatedly and painfully flashed into his mind.

(in)Visible

Joseph returned to his homeland of Congo and began to work with HEAL Africa, a faith-based hospital and clinic with whom we were collaborating on HIV prevention and care. One of Joseph's many tasks was to go into rebel-held territory to meet with the rebels. On his first trip he was captured by the rebels. They burned his vehicle and separated him from his coworkers, whom he never saw again. Joseph was kidnapped and taken to meet the rebel leader. He was told that he was going to be killed unless he could do two things—return with medicine to help the rebel soldiers, and bring Bibles in Kirwanda, their local language, for their wives. Joseph returned as he had promised. And in spite of being kidnapped two more times by different rebel leaders, he continues to enter rebel held territory to conduct a ministry of healing and forgiveness.

Joseph asked us for help. When women are raped, they are inflicted not only with emotional trauma and physical brutality but also HIV infection, sexually transmitted diseases, and in many cases pregnancy. It is the perpetrators' way of ensuring the permanent suffering of the women. We provided Joseph with post-exposure prophylaxis kits which can keep women from becoming infected with HIV. He worked with us on other HIV programs to ensure their quality.

We visited Joseph, his wife, also a nurse, and his family in their home and met Joseph's three children and their five newly adopted children, whose parents had died of HIV or were killed by rebels. They live in a wooden clapboard house with no running water but with love flowing among them. I see Joseph as a courageous ambassador of peace and hope. Joseph's vision is to have a home for more orphan children and provide them with education and healthcare.

I had an opportunity to invite Joseph to tell his story at a conference on Slavery and Poverty at First Presbyterian Church in Berkeley, California. Joseph had never been to the US and he said little about what he saw while he was visiting. But he did tell others "who he was." As Joseph engaged his audience, I watched the faces and eyes of those to whom he spoke. They heard him speak in broken English about the women who were kidnapped by the rebels and how he would call the rebel leader on the cell phone and tell them that he was coming for the women to return them to their families. Like the parable of the shepherd and the one lost sheep, he would go to rescue even one woman to bring her back to safety, leaving his own family and all else behind. He viewed these women not as strangers but as friends.

I watched as those who heard him were transformed by his stories and by the penetrating gaze of a courageous man who believed the teaching of Jesus. "There is no greater love than to give up your life for your friends." When asked why he does what he does in spite of being kidnapped and the constant threat of danger, Joseph replies, "I was born to serve. Serving is my vocation. It is not my business."

There is much that I learned from Joseph. I learned how intimately his vocation was entwined with forgiveness as he walked among the very people who were committing human atrocities. He was living out what I heard Abel, a theologian from Chad, say: "If your allegiance is to a nation, tribe, a political philosophy or an economic policy, and not to God, it allows you to separate yourself from another person and view them as inferior, no longer created in the image of God. And when that happens we can do dreadful things to that person." Joseph went into the forest and rescued kidnapped women from rebel soldiers. These women were obscure to the large aide organizations but not to Joseph. He viewed each woman as valuable whether a Hutu, Tutsi, Rwandan, or Congolese because he saw their value through the eyes of God. Those who view others as invisible or obscure will never discover the value of a person as God sees them.

Arthur's story of connecting with Joseph is clearly a moving example of a person who could have remained invisible without intentionally seeking him out. We talk about the impact this encounter has had on Arthur personally.

I look back at that unplanned and unanticipated encounter with Joseph Ciza, who at that time was an unknown nurse in what was initially to me an obscure and dangerous region of the world. Had I not conducted the workshop and had I not spoken to one of the healthcare workers in Goma, I would never have known about the life and work of Joseph. Nor would I have learned what he taught me in so few words—that the importance of a person is not in what they do, but who they are. It is extraordinary to me that in my many decades of education I had never stopped to think about what is most important to learn from an individual when we first meet them. The encounter with Joseph was an example of the importance of one individual and how one person, in a brief encounter, can alter how we continue the remainder of our life's journey. We must not look at their position, title, wealth, profession, or status as being the most important—rather we must discover who they really are.

I wonder if many of us will find a Joseph in our everyday journey. I suspect that we seldom know the impact we have in the lives of others. I can think of examples of this in literature and film. In fact, it reminds me of the Capra film "It's a Wonderful Life."

That's a good example. I believe the importance of one person, was the theme Frank Capra's movie, made way back in 1946. Capra said that he did not want to make yet another movie about World War II, a war that resulted in the death of over 56 million people. He wanted to focus on the importance of one individual and did so by showing George Bailey and what the world would have been like if he were not alive. Using flashbacks we get insight into all of the individuals who were touched by one person and the difference it made to the community in which he lived. Although fictional, it is a story that reminds us of the value of one person and why the loss of even one person can diminish the whole.

HOW SHALL WE LIVE?

Finding a person of value may mean that we need to be open to interruptions and the opportunities they present—something that may be difficult in our fast-paced society. We may think of life as an orderly series of events under our control, not realizing that an unwelcomed interruption may just be about introducing a new person into our life—whether it comes in the form of an acquaintance, a stranger, a detour into an illness, or some other crisis. We may later realize this was to be a transforming experience. When we look back in history, or travel forward through modern landscapes, we come to the inescapable conclusion that what matters most in life's journey is the individual. Whether a thousand years old or a thousand seconds old, all the technology, all the buildings, all the science, all the communication means nothing unless it all meets the fundamental needs of the individual. The risk of continuing on a trajectory away from the value of one, toward a system of depersonalization, is to risk being catapulted into the sphere of some new master who will seduce us into believing that everything that is organized, or big, or new, or fast, or technical is good while everything that is about the value of the one is meaningless. It will, in the end, divorce each one of us from the necessity of viewing each other as visible and valuable, and it will insert meaningless alternatives into societies, cultures, religion, and political agendas. Rein Staal, in an article on "The Forgotten Story of Postmodernity,"[14] quotes the writer Guardini, who spoke of the "divorce of power and person" as a warning against the loss of the importance of the person.

Staal also spoke of lessons that we must learn from the past as a caution against a headlong trajectory into modernism and its child, secularism. "After centuries of reductionism and debunking, personhood stood reduced to mere subjectivity, the transparent assertion of values without anchorage or horizon. Power cast a shadow over man through the impersonal institutions and processes following their own soulless logic." Modernism brought secularism to the forefront of human reason and along with it a divorce from the spiritual, as pointed out in Max Picard's book *The Flight from God*. Staal comments,

> Picard saw the modern secular West as a self-perpetuating system of spiritual amnesia, frantically busy yet accomplishing nothing, full of communication yet bereft of conversation; loud and bright, yet at the same time mute and senseless. Love, friendship, and loyalty exist only as fragments in the world of flight from God; evanescent snippets of experience that come and go. That is why, in modern times, words have become merely signs, disconnected from the persons who utter them.[15]

These are the pleas from writers and philosophers to preserve the value of the individual against the onslaught of secular systems that aggregate individuals into impersonal structures. The teachings of Jesus inform us

14. Rein Staal, "The Forgotten Story of Postmodernity," *First Things*, December 2008, online: http://www.firstthings.com/article/2008/11/004-the-forgotten-story-of-postmodernity.

15. Ibid.

of the value of the individual—no matter what the cost may be, the value of a person cannot be dismissed or destroyed. It is my hope and prayer that in recognizing the importance of the value of one, we may be able to throw off the shackles of culture, the mythology of science, the seduction of technology, and practices shrouded in politics and religion that foster depersonalization of the individual. Invest in a person and you will see justice, love, mercy and forgiveness. Invest in their transformation and you will promote eternal influence.

As we progress on our journey through life I am amazed and reassured at how many individuals I continue to meet who share the concept of the value of the individual. They too eagerly look forward to those who they will encounter in their personal journey who will bring unexpected fullness and richness into their lives. They are not alone in rejecting the avalanche of shallow communications in daily life. They too seek to find deeper meaning in individuals of value, even strangers, just as Paul found what he had longed for in Onesimus some two centuries ago.

We return to the central idea of our entire conversation, and really the whole book—"discovering" a person, once obscure and invisible to us, now transformed into one of importance and value. In the "mystery of one" we go deeper—raising the question, might we be placed here on earth to intersect with just one person in our entire lifetime? This arresting thought haunts me as being audacious, presumptuous, and even a bit frightening, but I cannot escape the possibility that God, in his plan, might well have placed me here for that one "invisible person." As I continue my journey I am forever altered by the concept of the "mystery of one."

THINK ON THESE THINGS

1. What is most mysterious to you about the concept of the "mystery of one"?

2. How would you explain the concept of the "mystery of one" in regard to those with whom you are closest—husband or wife, siblings, children, friends?

3. How does the concept of the "mystery of one" support or contradict the ministry of Jesus?

Epilogue

Paul's letter to Philemon is a story of the transformation of an individual. It is about Onesimus, the runaway slave, initially a stranger to Paul. The kind of transformation that occurred was not about greatness, achievement, or success. Nor was it about an expectation that God was going to take him to heights never before achieved. The transformation was a deeply personal experience that forever changed the relationship between the Apostle Paul and Onesimus and ultimately with Philemon. It began with an encounter between two unlikely people, under unlikely circumstances, and was recorded in a deeply personal but simple letter that documented the living out of the teachings of Jesus.

Paul had no idea what would happen to Onesimus as he sent him back to Philemon. If someone had told him or Philemon how the rest of the story of the life of Onesimus would play out, they would have been astonished. What happened next is not revealed in this short letter but can be pieced together from the dusty pages of obscure historical commentaries. The events that followed the return of this slave create the capstone for the concept laid out in this book and form the ultimate process of transformation

In the proverbial "rest of the story," Onesimus returns to Philemon, who fulfills Paul's request and emancipates the former slave, welcoming him as a "dear brother." Onesimus not only becomes a part of the house church there, but subsequently attains a leadership role. The crowning fact comes as tradition tells us of a person named Onesimus who became the bishop of Ephesus—from slave to bishop, obscurity to value.

The mystery of Paul's letter to Philemon is that it sets before us how God allows us to participate with him in the transformation of a person through the discovery of their value—a power that resides within each of us. Visible initially only to God himself, he then places the person in our path for his special purpose. The opportunity to engage with a person may be in an unlikely location, an inconvenient time, a moment or a decade, but no matter who, where, or when, the choice to participate lies with us.

ONE FINAL STORY—INVISIBLE JOSH

"You know, I am invisible." The stinging words came from the back of the car. Josh was safely belted into his seat. I was taking him home after a "play date" with my grandson, Leland.

In the afternoons, two days a week, I picked up Leland from his school. Josh and Leland, both seven years old, were friends from school. Josh always seemed to find me when I dropped Leland off at his classroom. He would approach me with his big blue eyes and a face that betrayed both hope and caution and would ask, "Can I have a play date with Leland today?" The first time he asked I told him that I would need to check with Leland's parents. When I did, I found that they were not enthused as they were leery as to just how much supervision children got at Josh's home. Josh persisted in his request and I could expect to see him every morning and afternoon for a week when he would ask, "Can I have a play date today?" I finally relented but said he had to come to our home and I would drive him home after they played.

When I drove Josh home he gave me careful directions. I was impressed with how precise he was for a seven year old. We talked about school and about his siblings. Josh then told me that his older brother beat him up a lot and took away his toys. "Doesn't your mom or dad stop him?" I asked. It was then that Josh said, "No, you know I am invisible." As he spoke I glanced in the rear view mirror and saw that his facial expression did not change as he spoke those words.

I could not shake his words loose. No child should ever grow up feeling invisible. Josh was surrounded by "things"—school, teachers, parents, siblings, and you name the technology aimed at children. Yet in the midst of all these things he felt invisible.

The rest of Josh's story remains unwritten, just as the story of Onesimus did when he was sent back to Philemon with uncertainty written all over his situation. Every "invisible" person who is discovered by some caring person moves through a process of transformation before coming out at the other side whole and valued. We can all take part in that important process.

As we were finalizing this book, we became increasingly aware of how many more individuals expressed feelings of invisibility and depersonalization. We asked ourselves, "Is this because in writing the book we have been constantly reminded of value and visibility in people's lives, or is it because invisibility is actually increasing in our culture?"

We ask you, our reader to take what you have read, reach out to those who surround you, and determine the answer yourself. Be it Josh or Fred, Mildred, George or Philippa—or any invisible friend or stranger—the rest of the story will be written by the hand of God.

VISIBLE

You called yourself invisible,
I beg to differ now.
I caught a sideways glimpse of you,
and began to see somehow,
a glimmer of a smile,
a dim light behind your frown—
I began to care and wonder,
who might have let you down.
You have been robbed of personhood,
you believed a lie
that you are not important—
your hopes and dreams did die.

(in)Visible

Somewhere along life's journey,
your world just fell apart—
you turned sad and bitter
and lost part of your heart.
I see your pain, I feel your hurt,
I hear your bleak despair,
I am drawn to speak, to reach, to touch,
and let you know I care.
You have value yet unseen,
a creation of God's hands—
He designed you for His love,
you must understand.
Come be my friend,
my sister, brother,
a precious one
I can discover.
Come believe—
receive the touch
of God who knows
and loves so much.
No longer invisible,
you can work and play,
and know that you have also,
blessed my life today.

—Barbara McLennan